DISCIPLINE THEM, LOVE THEM

PRACTICAL PROJECTS FOR PARENTS
by
Betty N. Chase

I. A BIBLICAL PATTERN OF CHILD DISCIPLINE

II. WAYS TO DISCIPLINE YOUR CHILD

III. BUILD SELF-ESTEEM IN YOUR CHILD

IV. THE MOST IMPORTANT THING YOU CAN DO FOR YOUR CHILD

The practical projects in this book also correlate to specific sessions in the course, *How to Discipline and Build Self-Esteem in Your Child* by Betty N. Chase, David C. Cook Publishing Co.

FOREWORD

by H. Norman Wright

For the past several years, it has been my privilege to know the work of Betty Chase. I have been impressed with her deep devotion to both thoroughness and practicality. It is my belief that her written work is both the finest researched material and the most Biblical in content of any materials that I have seen for parenting. If parents are serious in equipping themselves for the task and privilege of parenting, this resource has the potential for bringing about positive changes in parent-child relationships.

I'm delighted that this material is now available for parents.

INTRODUCTION

Don't just read this book!

It is a "doing" book—an exciting adventure of learning practical ways to apply the Biblical imperatives to discipline and build self-esteem in your children. As you complete each project you will experience life changes in your parenting.

At the heart of these 26 projects is a Biblical foundation of child rearing. God promises, "Correct thy son, and he shall give thee rest; yea, he shall give delight unto thy soul" (Prov. 29:17). The most important principle you need to know is how to shape your child's will without breaking his spirit, that is, a balance of building self-discipline *and* self-esteem in your child. Neglecting one of these areas will decrease your effectiveness in the other area.

These projects, when taken in order, will build the skills you need for a balanced approach.

In Part I you will discover what the Bible says about child rearing. It is a clear and positive approach to disciplining and building self-esteem.

As you complete Part II you will be developing the skills and methods of effective discipline which will help you have more control and enjoy your children more.

Part III will give you specific, practical ways to build self-esteem in your children. You will delight at the closer relationship that develops between you and them, and you will see your children become more confident themselves.

Select a schedule to follow as you work through these projects. You might ask your spouse, or find a friend or small group of friends who would also like to work through these parenting projects. You can meet once a week after completing various projects to share your insights and growth together.

This is a personal book. Write all of your responses to the projects in this book. Treat it like a workbook and freely write notes to yourself, underline important thoughts, etc., but be sure to do the projects in order because later projects are based on the skills you will learn in the earlier ones.

Before you begin, sit down and list two or three goals of what you would like to learn from your study. Then list two or three specific areas of child rearing that frustrate you now. Ask for your Heavenly Father's guidance and insights as you begin this rewarding adventure.

Betty Chase

DEDICATION

To my Father in Heaven who created me of clay—precious in His sight!

To my loving husband, Tom, who has encouraged me to be all that I could be.

To my son, John, who has motivated me to be sensitive to my impressions on his life because I love him!

A Piece of Clay

I took a piece of plastic clay
  And idly fashioned it one day.
And as my fingers pressed it still,
  It moved and yielded to my will.

I came again when days were past:
  The feel of clay was hard at last.
The form I gave it, it still bore,
  But I could change that form no more.

I took a piece of living clay
  And gently formed it day by day
And moulded with my press and art
  A young child's soft and yielding heart.

I came again when years were gone:
  It was a man I looked upon.
He still that early impress wore,
  And I could change it never more.

Anonymous

3

PART ONE

Do you want a wise child who is capable of making good choices in life and has self-control to deal with problems and temptations? If so, don't follow worldly philosophies of child discipline. The world will lead you astray in subtle ways. Whenever you read books and magazines or attend parent training sessions, always look at the aspects of child discipline that you are learning in light of what your Heavenly Father says in His guidebook for life—the Bible. God's plan for child discipline is clear, positive, and exciting to discover!

A BIBLICAL PATTERN OF CHILD DISCIPLINE

Project 1
What Do You Believe About Child Discipline?

Every parent has a philosophy of child discipline governing what he or she does or does not do in relation to his child. It may be conscious or unconscious, but it still operates.

Generally a parent either (1) disciplines like his parents disciplined him, or (2) reacts to his parents' style and uses an opposite approach. What is your philosophy? This first project will help you discover and verbalize it.

How did your father discipline you?

How did your mother discipline you?

What do you remember most about the times when your father disciplined you? Your mother?

Did your father or mother get angry when he or she disciplined you? ☐ Yes   ☐ No How did you feel if they did get angry?

What do you agree with about your parents' style of discipline?

What do you disagree with about your parents' style of discipline?

As you consider all of the above areas, how do you want to discipline your children?

Now consider where you feel your spouse may be coming from. What methods of discipline did your spouse's parents use with him or her?

What *similarities* do you see in the way your spouse disciplines and how he or she was disciplined as a child?

What *differences* do you see in the way your spouse disciplines and how he or she was disciplined as a child?

Generally, are you following your parents' style of discipline or have you reacted oppositely to your parents' style of discipline?

Generally, is your spouse following or reacting oppositely to his or her parents' style of discipline?

There are four general styles of discipline that parents can use. These four styles of discipline are based on two crucial factors:

(1) the amount of *control* the parents have over their child's behavior.

(2) the amount of *loving support* the parent gives to the child.

The chart below has two lines. The vertical lines represents the amount of love and support that is given to the child. The horizontal line represents the amount of control the parent has over the child's behavior. Read over the various combinations of control and loving support, which results in the four possible styles of discipline.[1]

Which do you think is the best style of discipline?
- ☐ Authoritarian
- ☐ Neglectful
- ☐ Authoritative
- ☐ Permissive

Which style of discipline did your mother use?

father?

Which style of discipline do you think you use?

your spouse?

Is there anything that you desire to change in your style of discipline? If so, what?

HIGH SUPPORT AND LOVE

Permissive Parent:
Does not try to control child's behavior; lets child do as he pleases; gives child too many choices and decisions without guidance; little correction when child doesn't behave; pleads with child to change behavior rather than commanding and making child change; is very loving to child; respects child as a person, listens, cares, gives focused attention; child feels loved in these areas.

Authoritative Parent:
Has high control over child's behavior; when he asks child to do something, he causes child to obey because he knows it's best for the child; believes a child is immature and needs direction; gives direction by control; very loving and supportive; spends time with child; listens to child; very concerned about meeting child's needs and helping child develop to his fullest potential.

LOW CONTROL OF BEHAVIOR

HIGH CONTROL OF BEHAVIOR

Neglectful Parent:
Has very little control over child's behavior; doesn't try to correct the child, lets him do what he wants; can be so involved in own affairs and problems that parent gives little attention to child; does not take time to really listen to child and encourage child; neglects emotional needs of child.

Authoritarian Parent:
Has very high control over child's behavior, causing child to comply with his demands and restrictions; makes child obey his rules and doesn't respect child's opinions, feelings, and needs; obedience is more important than the relationship; does not spend time listening to child; very little emotional support for the child.

LOW SUPPORT AND LITTLE LOVE

This book is designed to help you be an *authoritative* parent. To be an authoritative parent you must be a firm, effective disciplinarian and have high control over your children's behavior. But you must also be extremely loving and supportive to your children at the same time. The projects in this book will give you these two skills.

The part of the book that you are most interested in may be the area where you are already most comfortable and most skilled. So be sure to work through both the section on discipline and the section on building self-esteem in your children.

God will bless your adventure as you invest time in growing to be the best parent you can be!

What Does the Bible Say About Child Discipline?

I. What is the basic nature of a child?

Read each of the verses below and write the meaning in your own words.

"Behold, I was brought forth in [a state of] iniquity; my mother was sinful who conceived me [and I, too, am sinful]" (Ps. 51:5, AMP).

". . . The intent of man's heart is evil from his youth" (Gen. 8:21b, NASB).

"For all have sinned, and come short of the glory of God" (Rom. 3:23).

According to these verses, what is the basic nature of a child?

☐ A child is basically good.
☐ A child's heredity and environment will determine whether the child is basically good or evil.
☐ A child has a basic sin nature and will sin when left to follow his own ways.

II. What is childishness?

Read the following verses. Then write two or three sentences explaining what it means to be childish.

"When I was a child, I spake as a child, I understood as a child, I thought as a child: but when I became a man, I put away childish things" (I Cor. 13:11).

"Brethren, be not children (immature) in your thinking; continue to be babes in [matters of] evil, but in your minds be mature [men]" (I Cor. 14:20, AMP).

Look up Proverbs 22:15 and find another characteristic of childishness. What is it?

III. What is a child's role in the family?

Read each of the verses below and rewrite them in your own words.

"Children, obey your parents in the Lord: for this is right" (Eph. 6:1).

"Honour thy father and mother; which is the first commandment with promise; That it may be well with thee, and thou mayest live long on the earth" (Eph. 6:2, 3).

"Children, obey your parents in all things: for this is well pleasing unto the Lord" (Col. 3:20).

"It is good for a man that he bear the yoke in his youth" (Lam. 3:27).

"It is good for a young man to be under discipline, for it causes him to sit apart in silence beneath the Lord's demands" (Lam. 3:27, 28, TLB).

7

Write two or three sentences stating your conclusions about what a child's role and responsibility is in family relationships.

IV. Should parents exercise authority over their children?

Read the following verses and rewrite them in your own words, keeping the same meaning.

"He who spares his rod hates his son; But he who loves him disciplines him diligently" (Prov. 13:24, NASB).

"Discipline your son in his early years while there is hope. If you don't you will ruin his life" (Prov. 19:18, TLB).

"He [Moses] said to them, Set your [minds and] hearts on all the words which I command you this day, that you may command them to your children, that they may be watchful to do all the words of this law" (Deut. 32:46, AMP).

"Do not withhold discipline from the child; if you punish him with the rod, he will not die" (Prov. 23:13, NIV).

The Lord talking to Samuel about Eli: "For I have told him that I will judge his house forever for the iniquity which he knoweth; because his sons made themselves vile, and he restrained them not" (I Sam. 3:13).

A bishop then must be . . . "One that ruleth well his own house, having his children in subjection with all gravity; (for if a man know not how to rule his own house, how shall he take care of the church of God?)" (I Tim. 3:4, 5).

Considering all of the previous Scriptures, what does the Bible say about parents exercising authority over their children?

V. The inner attitude of one exercising authority.

I Peter 5:2,3 beautifully describes the inner attitude of one who has authority:

"I urge you then to see that your 'flock of God' is properly fed and cared for. Accept the responsibility of looking after them willingly and not because you feel you can't get out of it, doing your work not for what you can make, but because you are really concerned for their well-being. You should aim not at being 'little tin gods' but as examples of Christian living in the eyes of the flock committed to your charge." (I Peter 5:2, 3, Phillips)

Some people exercise authority as "little tin gods," ruling those under them selfishly. God desires that Christian parents use their authority for the well-being of their flock—not to make rules and set restrictions for their convenience only. A person in authority has the responsibility to love and serve those under him, exercising authority for their best interests.

There are also specific inner attitudes that are important in knowing how to exercise authority:

1) *Be motivated by love for those under you.* "All those whom I love I correct and discipline" (Rev. 3:19, Phillips).

2) *Be patient.* "He that is slow to anger appeaseth strife" (Prov. 15:18b).

3) *Have yourself under control.* "A man without self-control is as defenseless as a city with broken down walls" (Prov. 25:28, TLB).

4) *Don't be angry.* "An angry man stirreth up strife, and a furious man aboundeth in transgression" (Prov. 29:22).

5) *Have a soft tone of voice.* "A soft answer turneth away wrath: but grievous words stir up anger" (Prov. 15:1).

6) *Discipline with respect for your child.* "Fathers, provoke not your children to anger, lest they be discouraged" (Col. 3:21).

VI. What are the results if parents do not discipline their children?

Consciously or unconsciously, every parent is exercising a philosophy of discipline that includes (1) what he believes about the basic nature of a child, (2) how he looks at childishness, (3) what the child's role in the family is, (4) whether parents have the right to exercise authority over their children, and (5) with what inner attitudes that authority should be exercised. Your beliefs about these crucial issues determine your *actions* in *child discipline.*

The Bible explains to parents that they will reap what they sow if they don't correct their children. Some parents reap foolish sons. Foolish means silly, being unwise, exhibiting folly. The word *folly* means weakness of mind or an unprofitable undertaking.

A. *Read the following verses and circle the words that describe the feelings of the parents of a foolish son.*
"A foolish son is a grief to his father, and bitterness to her who bare him" (Prov. 17:25).

". . . the father of a fool hath no joy" (Prov. 17:21b).

B. *What causes a child to be foolish?*
"Foolishness is bound in the heart of a child; but the rod of correction shall drive it far from him" (Prov. 22:15).

What causes a child to be foolish?

What do you think foolishness is in children? (See definition above.)

How does a child get wiser and lose his foolish ways?

9

C. *Circle the words that describe what kind of child becomes foolish and brings shame to his mother.*

". . . a child who gets his own way brings shame to his mother" (Prov. 29:15, NASB).

D. *Circle the words that describe what parents should do if they have a child who is foolish and who brings them grief and shame.*

"A wise servant shall have rule over a son that causeth shame" (Prov. 17:2).

Benefit for the Child	Benefit for the Parents
"Foolishness is bound in the heart of a child; but the rod of correction shall drive it far from him" (Prov. 22:15).	"Correct thy son, and he shall give thee rest" (Prov. 29:17a).
"Train up a child in the way he should go: and when he is old, he will not depart from it" (Prov. 22:6)	
"The rod and reproof give wisdom: but a child left to himself bringeth his mother to shame" (Prov. 29:15).	"Correct thy son, and . . . he shall give delight unto thy soul" (Prov. 29:17b).
"Chasten thy son while there is hope" (Prov. 19:18a).	

III. What are the positive results if parents discipline their children?

To be wise means to discern and judge soundly what is true or false and what is proper or improper. Wisdom includes discernment, sound judgment, and discretion.

Read the following verse and circle the words that describe feelings that the parents of a wise child have.

"The father of the righteous shall greatly rejoice: and he that begetteth a wise child shall have joy of him" (Prov. 23:24).

What gives a child wisdom?

"The rod and reproof give wisdom: but a child left to himself bringeth his mother to shame" (Prov. 29:15).

According to this verse, what two things bring wisdom to a child?

_____and

_____

The Lord promises several specific benefits in a home where the children are corrected and disciplined. Read each of the verses in the chart above and *circle*

the words or phrases that name the benefit either for the child or for the parent.

Proverbs 29:17 has two promises for parents. Let's look at them in more detail.

"Correct thy son, and he shall give thee rest; yea, he shall give delight unto thy soul."

What does *rest* mean to you?

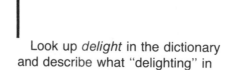

Look up *delight* in the dictionary and describe what "delighting" in your child means.

Why would a parent delight in his child if he corrects him?

Write a paragraph summarizing what the Bible says about child discipline.

A Biblical Pattern of Discipline_

Does God, our Heavenly Father, discipline His children? If so, what principles does *He* follow? In this project we will discover the answers to these questions. We will also discover the purpose of discipline, the goal of discipline, the proper inner attitude of the disciplinarian, and the results of discipline.

Where will we find all this? In our Guidebook to life—the Bible! God has not left us without direction in this crucial area.

Begin by reading Hebrews 12:5-13 carefully. (Please use a translation [King James, New American Standard, Revised Standard, etc.] and not a paraphrase for this study.)

Write the main idea of Hebrews 12:5-13 in one sentence:

Now look at the passage more closely and answer the following questions:

Who does God discipline (vss. 5 and 8)?

What is God's motivation in disciplining His children according to verse 6?

What is your position before God if you are not disciplined (vs. 8)?

Therefore, according to verse 8, discipline is a sign of _____

_____

_____

in the family of God.

What is the resulting attitude in children when their earthly fathers discipline them (vs. 9)?

Why does God discipline His children (vs. 10)? Write down the words from this verse and then explain them.

What kind of feelings exist in a situation requiring discipline according to verse 11?

What is the end result of being disciplined? (Vs. 11; *note: Yieldeth* means "to give back.")

Define "fruit of righteousness" (vs. 11).
   fruit:

   righteousness:

11

Why do you think the descriptive word "peaceable" is used in verse 11?

Looking at verses 12 and 13, locate the parts of the body that are mentioned and then the words that describe that part.

As our Heavenly Father looks at us, He sees weak parts of us. There are character traits, personality traits, and weaknesses in our soul that need to be healed. Sometimes no one else can see those weak parts (and sometimes they do!). Sometimes we don't know our own weaknesses. But God, in His love, wants us whole. So, at times, He uses discipline to help us be aware of those weak parts and want to change. He can heal those weak parts and loves us so much that He does.

Fill in Part A and then Part B of the following chart, paralleling how parents would discipline their children if they followed God's pattern of discipline.

As you read over Part B of the

FOLLOWING GOD'S PATTERN OF DISCIPLINE

Part A
Our Heavenly Father and His Children

Looking over the previous questions, put these ideas (and any others you see in Hebrews 12:5-13) into statement form. Each statement should contain a principle of how or why God disciplines His children. List at least seven; there are more.

1. God disciplines His children because He loves them (vs. 5).
2.

3.

4.

5.

6.

7.

Part B
Parents and Their Children

After you have completed the principles of discipline in Part A of this chart, reword each of the statements, stating it in terms of parent-child relationships. (See sample below.)

1. Parents discipline their children because they love their children.
2.

3.

4.

5.

6.

7.

chart, select two statements that you feel are the most important ones for you to remember in your family at this time. Write each principle below and then your reason for selecting it.

Principle 1:

Reason why I chose this principle:

Principle 2:

Reason why I chose this principle:

What is a child like who has very few limits or no limits at all? Describe one that you know or have seen.

What do you think are some of the *feelings* that a child with very few limits or little discipline experiences?

Do you feel your children have enough limits? too many? or a good balance? Why?

List some positive qualities or results that you see in your children's lives *that have come as a result of your discipline.*

Child's Name: _____
1.

2.

3.

Child's Name: _____
1.

2.

3.

Note: For each exercise like this in the book, where you are asked to analyze each child separately, use an additional sheet of paper if you have more children.

What are some weak areas in your children's lives that need correcting?

Child's Name: _____
1.

2.

3.

Child's Name: _____
1.

2.

3.

After each of the above weaknesses, write one positive thing you can do as a parent to correct that weakness. Discipline is a painful thing, but God has given us a positive, loving pattern to follow, resulting in many benefits for our children, as well as for you as a parent!

13

What Is the Difference Between Discipline and Punishment?

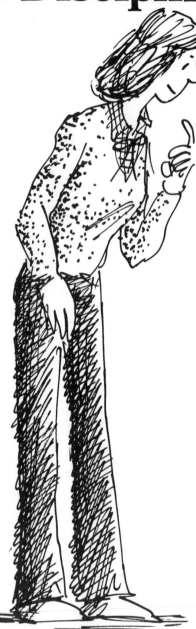

defined as training that develops self-control. Discipline includes three levels.

Level 3	Correction
Level 2	Training
Level 1	Instruction

The foundational level of discipline, Level 1, is *instruction*. Discipline begins with instructing and teaching your children.

Both the Old Testament and New Testament word for discipline support this definition containing all three levels. However, the word *discipline* in the English language is evolving to eliminate the "instruction" and just mean correction or training.

Level 2 is *training*. Training means to lead and direct the growth of the child. It includes helping the child form habits and develop proficiency in his instruction.

Level 3 is *correction*. Correction means to alter or adjust a child's behavior by taking action to cause him to follow previous instruction.

Therefore, correction follows instruction. A child needs correction when he knows your instructions and doesn't follow them.

It is crucial to take action at this level or your child's sense of security and growth in self-control will be damaged. Being direct and assertive at this level is important. There are several specific methods of correction you can use. You will learn about each specific method in this book.

Describe a time when you began to correct your child (Level 3) and then discovered that he had not really understood your rules or instruction (Level 1).

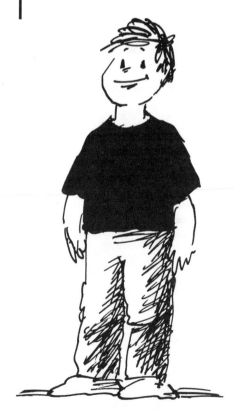

I. What is discipline?

Usually discipline is thought of in very negative concepts. Discipline, in the true sense of the word is positive, encouraging, and even proof of love, as we discovered in Hebrews 12.

The root word of discipline is *disciple*. You are making disciples of your children. Discipline is

Write down a short description of the last time you had to correct one of your children and what you were correcting.

PUNISHMENT AND DISCIPLINE		
	Punishment	**Discipline**
Purpose	To inflict penalty for an offense	To train for correction and maturity
Focus	Past misdeeds	Future correct deeds
Attitude	Hostility and frustration on the part of the parent	Love and concern on the part of the parent
Resulting Emotion in the Child	Fear and guilt	Security

In the situation above, describe when and how you instructed your child in that area previous to the time of correction.

II. Contrasting Discipline and Punishment

In the original language of the Bible there was a difference in the meanings of the words *discipline* and *punishment.* Parents are instructed to discipline their children, but they are not instructed to punish their children.

What's the difference?

As stated earlier, the root word of discipline is *disciple* and means learner. The definition of discipline in both the Old and New Testament involves instruction and training, as well as correcting. Discipline is to be motivated by love and concern, according to Hebrews 12.

In contrast, punishment implies getting even, retaliation, vengeance, and exacting a penalty.

Dr. Bruce Narramore, in his excellent book, *Help! I'm a Parent,* differentiates between discipline and punishment in the chart on page 16.[1]

Study this chart and write a paragraph describing in your own words the differences between discipline and punishment. List as many as you can.

A parent's inner attitude while disciplining is crucial. It is possible for a parent to use one method of correction and be either disciplining or punishing depending on the parent's inner attitude.

Children are very sensitive to an adult's inner attitude towards them. In fact, a child can many times detect anger on the part of the parent when the parent does not know that he is angry.

As parents, we all get angry sometimes because raising children is not an easy task and children have a way of trying parents. If your child has just disobeyed you and needs correction, and you are angry, what do you usually do?

Knowing how to handle anger is a necessary skill so that parents can discipline their children and not punish (get even with) their children.

Try some of the following suggestions when you get angry:

1. Don't lash out to correct immediately. Don't hit your child anywhere on his body—arm, leg, face, etc. (There is a difference between *hitting* and *spanking*.) It is also dangerous to use spanking as a method of discipline when your anger is out of control. That can lead to child abuse.

2. Separate yourself from the child for a few minutes.

3. Admit to yourself that you are angry and ask the Lord to help you deal with your anger and gain control.

4. Ask the Lord to help you discern why you are angry. Sometimes it's at yourself because you let the situation go on so long without correction. Take action. (As you work through this book, you will gain skills in taking action.)

5. When you are calm, go to your child and then take action to correct him.

When you were disciplined as a child did your father or mother usually get angry with you when he or she disciplined you?

Father: ☐ Yes ☐ No
Mother: ☐ Yes ☐ No

How did you feel if your parents disciplined you in anger?

When was the last time you were angry with one of your children? Describe why and what happened.

How did you handle your anger?

What improvements do you see that you could make in the area of handling anger?

If you have disciplined your child with uncontrolled anger, the best way to make it right is to ask your child to forgive you—not for correcting him, but for being angry while you disciplined him.

Shaping a Child's Will Without Breaking His Spirit

A Warning to Parents . . .

"Fathers, provoke not your children to anger, lest they be discouraged" (Col. 3:21).

The Bible has many verses to parents about the importance of disciplining and correcting children. But a warning stands out among these verses on child rearing. What does this verse mean? How can parents provoke children to anger?

First, note that the word "fathers" means parents—those who are raising children, both mothers and fathers. "Provoke not your children to anger" means that there are things which parents can do that stimulate anger in their children.

Think back over your childhood. What were some things adults did to you that caused you to get angry? (Time yourself for two minutes and write down everything that comes to your mind. For example: being unfair.)

1.

2.

3.

4.

5.

6.

7.

The following are ways parents can provoke children to anger. Your list may include some of these:

yelling
embarrassing or ridiculing
ignoring child; being too busy; not listening
disciplining or striking child in anger
not caring for child's needs
comparing or showing favoritism
impatience
lack of sensitivity
using a harsh tone of voice
name-calling
too many rules; not enough rules
pretending to be perfect
lying to a child; not keeping promises
overreacting
overprotecting
not respecting privacy
demanding perfection; too high expectations
falsely accusing; jumping to conclusions
teasing
disciplining in front of others
parental fighting; making a child take sides
interrupting
inconsistency
failing to discipline
lack of trust
inflexibility
punishment which is unjust, too harsh, or unfair
threats without discipline; nagging
giving tasks beyond child's ability
not answering questions; not explaining
critical; always seeing bad
talking about child's faults
denial of requests without consideration
not forgiving
not respecting child's decisions
conditional acceptance

Ask the Lord to help you identify *one* area mentioned above that you need to work on in your parent-child relationships. Name the specific behavior towards your child that you desire to change:

Now, write a prayer to God, (use a separate sheet of paper) asking Him to help you be aware when you are provoking your children in this way during the next seven days and to help you eliminate it from your relationships with your children.

Look at the second half of Colossians 3:21. When a parent provokes a child to anger, the result in the child is . . .

The word *discouraged* means to lose heart, to be spiritless, dismayed, to have no courage. When a person is discouraged it means that they just don't have the heart to go on; they give up.

Describe a time in your life when you have been discouraged for any reason, either as an adult or as a child.

Write two to four words describing your feelings at that time.

Write two to four words describing your reactions to life and those around you during that time.

What was your general outlook during this discouraging time?

Think of a specific time when you saw one of your children discouraged. Describe that child's feelings, actions, responses, and general outlook on life during that time of discouragement.

Child:

Age:

Situation:

Child's feelings:

Child's actions during that time:

Child's responses and general outlook on life:

What signs could you look for in your children that would indicate that they have been discouraged by your method or manner of discipline?

If you discover that you have done things to provoke your children to anger, there is no quicker way to restore the

	CHILD'S WILL	CHILD'S SPIRIT
Definition	A child's ability to set his own goals, desires, and actions, either in accordance with, or contrary to, the will of his parents.	An abstract part of a child that is aware of being a unique individual and has a need to be respected as a person.
Child's Need	A child can choose either to be his own boss and do what he wants or submit to his parent's will. A child has a need to be molded and guided and given wisdom in his life (despite the child's attempts to be his own boss).	A child has a need to be respected as a person and as a unique creation of God's.
Description	The strength of a child's will varies from being easily guided and compliant to exercising extreme self-will with a strong determination to be his own boss. A child's will can be astoundingly strong!	The spirit is tender, delicate, fragile, and sensitive. It can be easily broken.
Parent's Responsibility	To shape and mold his child's will; to stop child when he goes his own way and take action to correct child.	To build child's self-esteem, giving total respect to child as a person.

relationship than to ask for forgiveness. If we are humble enough to admit that we are not perfect, we strengthen our relationships with our children.

Even if your children are teenagers and God shows you an area where you have provoked your teens since they were children, ask for forgiveness. God can bring healing and newness in the relationship. Parents who have applied this verse in their families have seen years of healing take place!

Summary of Part I

All the verses that we have studied so far fall into two categories: (1) parents need to correct and discipline their children, and (2) parents should not break their child's spirit and discourage them. In other words, *shape your child's will without breaking his spirit.*

Study the chart on page 18. Which column do you relate to and understand the most?
- ☐ Child's will
- ☐ Child's spirit

Neglecting one area will affect adversely the other area. A parent who builds self-esteem, but does not discipline a child, cannot build their child's self-esteem to the fullest because lack of discipline tears down the esteem of a child. So, follow the Biblical imperatives to parents, with equal emphasis on both aspects of child rearing.

One of the most delicate skills in parenting is distinguishing between a child's will and his spirit. How does a parent do this?

First, by having good strong

practical handles on *disciplining* and *building self-esteem*. These will be presented in Part II and Part III of this book. Second, by continuing to analyze which aspect of the child you are dealing with in a conflict—the will or the spirit.

The following exercise may help you as you analyze which aspect of your child you are dealing with.

Write the name of the child with whom you have had the most conflicts lately:

_____Age _____

Describe three situations lately where you tried to correct that child. *Describe situations where (1) you felt you needed to set limits on the child's behavior, and (2) the child became emotional or angry or refused to comply.*

Situation 1
What was the conflict about?

What did *you* do or say?

Child's reactions:

As you consider this situation, which is involved in this conflict?
- ☐ Child's broken spirit
- ☐ Child's strong will

Situation 2
What was the conflict about?

What did *you* do or say?

Reactions of child:

What was the issue?
- ☐ Child's broken spirit
- ☐ Child's strong will

Situation 3
What was the conflict about?

What did *you* do or say?

Child's reactions:

What was the issue?
- ☐ Child's broken spirit
- ☐ Child's strong will

Do you notice any significant patterns in the conflicts?

PART TWO

WAYS TO DISCIPLINE YOUR CHILD

Project 6

Are You Disciplining on All Three Levels?

When you think of discipline, what is the first word or phrase that comes to your mind? Usually, one thinks of correction or a means of correction, such as spanking.

Correction is part of discipline, but not all of it. As we learned earlier, discipline has three levels and correction is only one of those levels. Study the following chart which defines and describes each level of discipline in detail.

LEVELS OF CHILD DISCIPLINE		
	Definition	**Specific ways to accomplish this level of discipline**
Level 1 Instruction	To impart knowledge or information; to furnish with direction by modeling, teaching, and commanding (giving orders).	Modeling by parent. Parent lives the standards he sets and is an example. Informal instruction. Parent uses everyday occurrences and situations as opportunities to informally instruct and share his own values and standards. Formal instruction. Setting aside specific time(s) for the purpose of instructing and teaching children.
Level 2 Training	To help a child form habits and develop proficiency in areas in which he has been instructed.	Doing things with the child and instructing him while you are doing them together. Teaching a more complex task or concept, one step at a time. Talking about an issue so that further depth of knowledge can be gained and misconceptions cleared up. Determining child's abilities in relationship to the skill you are teaching him. Rewards are a very effective method to use on the training level.

Level 3 Correction	To alter or adjust a child's behavior by taking action to cause him to follow previous training and instruction.	Select one or more of the following methods of correction:
		
		  Direct, assertive communication
		  Spanking
		  Natural consequences
		  Logical consequences
		  Extinction

Discipline begins on Level 1, progresses to Level 2, and when and if Level 3 is necessary, it is exercised. That's how children are taught and retain values for life. Each level is the foundation for the next.

Level 3 Correction

Level 2 Training

Level 1 Instruction

In the chart below list five specific behaviors you expect from each of your children—rules you have, manners, chores, school conduct and grades, limits on freedom, etc. (Make a similar chart on separate paper for each child.)

Then look at each level of discipline and check whether you have dealt with that behavior by instructing and by training. If possible, list specific times of instruction and training. After instruction and training, has the child needed correction in that area? If so, check Level 3 also.

Do you see any areas where you have corrected your child, but failed to instruct him? If so, what area?

Read over the lists that you made of expectations in behavior for your other children. Circle any areas that you desire to further teach or train.

What are some qualities that are important for a parent to have while training a child?

When you need to correct your child, what methods have you been using?

Usually parents struggle more with correcting a child than with teaching and training him. Correction is much easier if parents have a handle on specific methods. The more skilled you are at correcting your child, the less correcting is necessary and the more peaceful moments there will be for teaching and training. The next several projects will teach you specific, practical skills in how to correct your child.

Specific behavior that I expect from _____ _____ (child's name) (age)	Level 1 Instruction	Level 2 Training	Level 3 Correction

If You Want Action, Take Action!

When a parent wants his children to change their behavior, he usually tells the children what he wants. Sometimes parents talk and talk and never "do" anything. Children respond to action, but most of the time they do not respond to words until they know you will take action, if necessary.

1. A picture of a parent's behavior to correct children could look like this:

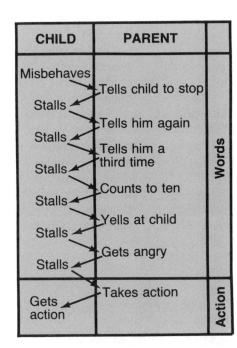

2. Think back when you were a child. Describe what your parents did before they crossed the line and took *action* to correct you.

3. Ask your spouse or an intimate friend to describe your behavior before you take action in disciplining your children.

Ask them to observe you and identify what words you are using before you take action. Have them fill out the accompanying chart similar to the former sample.

Spouse's/friend's description:

CHILD	PARENT	
Misbehaves		Words
		Action

According to your spouse's/

friend's assessment, how many times do you use words before you take action?

If you use words a lot before you take action, answer the following:
Describe the progression of your feelings each time you use words again to solve the problem.

How do you usually feel when you are taking action?

When do your children change their behavior—when you are using words or when you take action?
Do you see any changes that you desire to make about where you want to draw the line between using words and taking action? If so, what?

What kind of action can a parent take to change his child's behavior? There are several methods of correction that you can use. You will be given the skills to use these methods in the projects in this section.
But remember: **If you want a change in your children's actions you'll need to take action yourself. Once your children believe that you will take action, you will not need to take that action as often. They will more readily obey your words!**

Method 1: Direct Assertive Communication

When parents need to discipline their children, one of several "actions" can be used:

- Communication
- Spanking
- Logical Consequences
- Natural Consequences
- Rewards
- Extinction

I. ALWAYS use communication as your first method of discipline.

It is a preventative method and may solve the problem.

Why should parents use communication first to solve problems?

1. Using communication first gives the child the benefit of the doubt and treats him with respect.

2. Communication is necessary to evaluate whether the child understood the instruction. A parent can find this out by asking, "What is our rule?" or "What did I ask you to do?" As the child reflects back your instruction, you gain insight into which level of discipline you are dealing with—instruction, training, or correction.

3. Sometimes communication can prevent misbehavior at the level of "talk." However, at times it will not be enough to solve the problem and a second method of correction will need to be used.

II. What is communication?

Communication consists of sharing information and exchanging opinions or thoughts. As information is shared, each person understands the other.

There are three aspects of communication necessary to give . . .

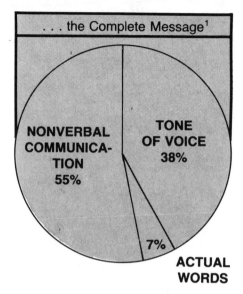

... the Complete Message[1]

NONVERBAL COMMUNICA-TION 55%

TONE OF VOICE 38%

7%

ACTUAL WORDS

It is amazing but true that we communicate much more by our tone of voice and nonverbal communication than by the words we use. So remember that your child will respond to all three aspects of communication as you correct him and that your tone of voice and nonverbal communication will reveal more about how you feel than your words will tell.

III. What kind of communication do you want to relay while correcting?

This project will focus on increasing your ability to be *direct* and *assertive*. When you are correcting your children, your communication needs to be clear, not vague, so that children can comply with your expectations.

A. *Tone of voice*

Use a firm tone of voice—but not harsh. Let your tone of voice state that you mean what you say the very *first* time you ask your child to change his behavior.

If you are angry, your tone of voice will be harsh, loud, and angry. Loudness and harshness is not necessary to get a child to change his behavior. However, a *firm* tone of voice is necessary—especially for a strong-willed child.

B. *Nonverbal communication*

Practice the following nonverbal communication while disciplining.

Eye contact:	Look directly into the child's eyes. (If the child is small, get on his level.) Ask for eye contact, if necessary.
Body posture:	Lean towards child.
Distance:	Close to child. (Do not communicate with child who is walking away from you. Say, lovingly, "Come here.")
Facial Expressions:	Relaxed and friendly.

C. *Words*

1. *Don't state wishes and desires when you need to make a command.*

Don't say:	"I would like you to stop biting your baby brother."
Do say:	"Stop biting your baby brother."

2. *Describe in detail what you want.*

Don't say:	"Act right."
Do say:	"Stop jumping on the sofa, and put your feet on the floor."

3. *Don't beg, plead, or count.*

Don't say: "Come for dinner. . . . I

said, Come for dinner! . . . I'm going to count to ten and you better come . . . 1 . . . 2 . . . 3 . . . 4 . . . 5 . . . (etc.)."

Do say: "Come for dinner right now." (If child does not come, state the next action that you will take if he doesn't come now.)

4. *Do not use rhetorical questions; instead begin requests with words like: I want . . . I will not . . . Our rule is . . . I need you to . . .*

Don't say: "Don't you think you should go to bed now?" "Wouldn't you like to go to bed now?" "It's late. How about going to bed now?"

Do say: "I want you to go to bed now. Our rule is bedtime at 8:30."

5. *Make your request once, expecting a change in the child's behavior. Don't make the same request over and over.*

Don't say: "Please shut the door, Mike." (Mike does not shut door.) "Mike, I asked you to shut the door." (Mike does not shut door.) "Would you *please* do as I asked?" (Mike does not shut door.)

Do say: "Please shut the door, Mike." (Mike does not shut door. Do not make the request again.)

6. *If the child does not respond to communication, state the action you will take, if necessary.* You are moving from communication to a second method of discipline.

Do Say: "Please shut the door, Mike." (Mike does not shut the door.) "If you do not shut the door right now, you will need to stay inside the rest of the day and not use the door."

7. *Don't make empty threats—take actions that you say you will.*

Don't say: "I'm going to spank you if you don't stop." (Child doesn't stop.) "I said, stop that or you're going to get a spanking!" (Child doesn't stop.) "Do you want a spanking?"

Do say: "I'm going to spank you if you don't stop." (Child doesn't stop.)

"Come with me." (Spank child.)

8. *Don't give the child choices or consequences that you don't really mean.*

Don't say: (At 11 a.m.) "You can either put your toys away, or go to bed for the rest of the day."
(Choice)

Do say: "You can either put your toys away or go to bed until you are ready to pick them up and put them away."

Don't say: "If you don't put your toys away, you won't be able to play with them for a week!"
(consequence)

Do say: "If you don't put your toys away, you will not be able to play with them for the rest of the day."

Using the eight principles above, read each of the statements below and write the number of the principle that is being violated. (Some statements may have more than one response.)

___ 1. "Don't you think you should brush your teeth this morning?"
___ 2. "Don't act like an animal!"
___ 3. "Jason, please get into the car so we can go. Please . . ."
___ 4. "I wish you would stop hitting Joey."
___ 5. "Don't you think you should stop eating so much?"
___ 6. "Come here, Susie . . . Don't run from me. . . . Susie! I *said* come here! Just wait until you come back!"
___ 7. "Can't you dress decently?"
___ 8. "If you break one more toy,

25

I won't ever buy you a toy again!"

___ 9. "I've asked three times now that you go to bed."

___ 10. "If you don't stop that, you'll have to come and sit by me. . . ." (Child doesn't stop. Mother does not make child sit by her.)

___ 11. "If you're not here by the time I count to five: One . . . two . . . three . . . four . . . four and a half. . . ."

___ 12. "I sure wish you would empty that kitchen wastebasket. It's overflowing with trash!"

___ 13. "You can either stop crying and carrying on, or we'll forget taking you to the dentist and your teeth can rot in your mouth!"

___ 14. "Close the door, Stevie. . . . Did you hear me? I said to close the door! . . . Would you shut that door? . . . I am so mad! You better shut that door NOW!"

(The answers to this exercise are on page 110. Please check your answers.)

List any rules that you have been unconsciously violating and want to work on.

Select one specific rule or goal to work on during the next seven days, and write that rule or goal here.

Ask your spouse or a close friend to be alert to situations during the next week when you are correcting your children. At the end of seven days, ask your spouse/friend to evaluate your verbal communication by the eight principles.

Method 2: Spanking

I. What does the Bible say about spanking?

Paraphrase each verse in your own words. (Note: in each verse, the word *rod* in Hebrew means "stick or branch from a tree.")

"The rod and reproof give wisdom: but a child left to himself bringeth his mother to shame" (Prov. 29:15).

"Foolishness is bound in the heart of a child; but the rod of correction shall drive it far from him" (Prov. 22:15).

"He that spareth his rod hateth his son: but he that loveth him chasteneth him betimes" (Prov. 13:24).

From the above verses, write your conclusion about what the Bible says about spanking as a method of child discipline.

II. Principles to remember about spanking

A. Do not spank in anger. When your anger is not controlled, *never* spank a child. It is dangerous!

B. Generally, spanking is used more with toddlers and preschoolers, but it is also used with elementary-age children. It should be completed by age 8 to 11. Teenagers should never be spanked.

C. Use spanking when a young child openly defies your authority. When you tell your preschooler to come to you and he runs away from you, that is open defiance.

D. Don't be afraid to use spanking when it is the best method to use, but don't use spanking for every misbehavior. Spanking is one method of correction, but there are several other methods available, also. Carefully select your method of correction for each situation.

E. Spanking is a procedure. Don't reach out and hit a child; it is disrespectful. Take the child in a private place and then follow the seven steps listed below. The only exception to this is when a child is too young to spank and just beginning to learn the meaning of the word *no.* This is done by saying no and hitting the back of his hand; the child learns to associate pain with the word *no.* This can be done with children between 9 and 18 months old. With older toddlers, begin following the seven steps listed below.

How to Spank

1. Get alone with the child; do not publicly embarrass him.
2. Ask "What is our rule?" or "What did Daddy (or Mommy) say?" You are making sure the child understood your instruction before you correct him.
3. Ask "What did you do?" You are asking him to establish personal responsibility for his actions and confess. This is important.
4. Explain that you love him and equate love with correction. Say, "I love you and want to help you learn how to do the right thing next time."
5. Spank the child. Give him a few swift, but painful swats on the buttocks. The child's angry, mad cry should change to a softer, giving-in cry.
6. Comfort the child immediately after spanking. Do not reject the child. Hold the child close and reassure him of your love. Only the parent who spanks is the one to do the comforting.
7. If necessary, have the child make restitution.

A parent's conversation during these seven steps might sound like this:

(Place child on your lap.) "Timmy, what did Mommy say about throwing your ball in the house?" . . . "Yes that's right, no ball playing in the house. But what did you do?" . . . "Yes, you disobeyed the rule. What happens when you disobey Mommy or Daddy?" . . . "That's right, we give you a spanking. We love you, Timmy, and want to help you learn how to obey and do what's right. A spanking now will help you to remember to do the right thing the next time." . . . (Lay child over lap, and give a few brief, but painful swats on the buttocks until Timmy stops his angry cry and cries softly. Return child to your lap and hold him close. Be quiet a moment to allow for crying) . . . "Timmy, are you sorry you disobeyed Mommy and threw the ball in the house?" . . . "Good, I'm glad, and I forgive you. Now, sweep up the broken glass from the picture that fell down when the ball hit it. I'll hold the dustpan."

III. Applying this method of discipline

Scripture specifically refers to spanking as one way parents should correct their children, but it doesn't give a lot of details. Like most things, spanking can be *used* or *abused,* can have a *good effect* or a *negative effect,* can be carried out *appropriately* or *inappropriately.*

A. In the following sets of misbehaviors, choose which one in each set warrants a spanking.

1. ☐ Four-year-old Jessie spills her milk at supper while reaching for the butter.
   ☐ Four-year-old Jessie spills her milk at supper while reaching for the butter, after Daddy has told her twice to ask for what she wants.

Reason for selection:

2. ☐ Five-year-old David yells, "No, I won't!" when his mother tells him to come back and take his water toys out of the bathtub.
   ☐ Mother tells five-year-old David to take his toys out of the bathtub; David says "OK" but ten minutes later they're still there.

Reason for selection:

3. ☐ Three-year-old Lizzie discovers Mommy's lipstick and makeup; Mommy discovers Lizzie.

☐ Lizzie has been told not to touch anything on Mommy's dresser; Mommy discovers Lizzie with lipstick on.

Reason for selection:

What was the common denominator which warrants spanking in these examples?

(Check on page 110 to see if you found the common denominator.)

B. Case studies. Read each of the following case studies and then list the problem areas in each case study. There are several answers for each.

CASE STUDY 1

Melanie doesn't want to put on her snow pants when Mommy comes to pick her up at nursery school. She kicks her legs, says "NO!" emphatically. Mommy promises her a lollipop if she'll cooperate. Melanie still won't put on the snow pants. Mommy threatens to go home without her and pretends to leave. Melanie holds out. Mommy finally comes back and carries her out to the car without putting on the snow pants. In the car, Mommy, who is angry now, tells Melanie she's a rotten little girl.

Problem areas in Case Study 1:
1.

2.

3.

CASE STUDY 2

Jack and Sue are playing tag in the house. They bump into a windowsill and send one of Mommy's favorite plants crashing to the floor. Mommy, upset about her plant, shakes Sue roughly while yelling and screaming at her. Jack tries to escape, but Mommy manages to whack him a good one on the behind before he makes it out of the door. Upset, Mommy cries in the living room; Jack and Sue stay out of her way all afternoon.

Problem areas in Case Study 2:
1.

2.

3.

CASE STUDY 3

Twelve-year-old Bill is bouncing his basketball in the house. Dad asks him to stop. A little later Dad hears it again. Dad marches in, makes Bill bend over his bed and gives him three whacks with his belt while Bill's nine-year-old brother watches. Bill is stony-faced until Dad leaves. Then he says to his brother, "Ha! That didn't hurt."

Problem areas in Case Study 3:
1.

2.

3.

(See answers to case studies on page 110.)

IV. Application for you and your family.

Spanking should never be used as a punishment; it should be used only to correct. (See Project 4 if you need to review the difference between discipline and punishment.)

Have you ever used spanking with your children? Why, or why not?

When you were a child, were you ever spanked in anger?
☐ Yes ☐ No. If yes, how did you feel?

When you were a child, were you ever spanked and loved so much that all through the spanking you knew there was no anger present,

29

just love?

☐ Yes. If yes, how did you feel?

☐ No. If you check no, do you believe it is possible to spank in love? Why, or why not?

If you have not experienced correction with the rod in love, *do you believe the Bible* when it says, "The rod and reproof give wisdom" (Prov. 29:15) and "He that spareth his rod hateth his son" (Prov. 13:24)? The Hebrew word for *rod,* remember, means a stick or branch from a tree.

Describe the last time you spanked one of your children.
Child's name: _____
 Age: _____
What was the offense?

Were you angry? ☐ Yes ☐ No If yes, how did you handle your anger?

Was there a deliberate disobedience to a clear instruction, defiance of your authority, or deceit or lying when the child knew he shouldn't be doing or saying what he did?
☐ Yes ☐ No

Why do you think spanking was the best method of correction for the situation?

How do you know the child understood your instructions?

Did the child confess that he was wrong? ☐ Yes ☐ No

What did you say to the child that conveyed your deep love for him?

How did the child respond to the spanking?

Did you sense brokenness and repentance? ☐ Yes ☐ No If yes, how did you sense it?

Did you comfort the child immediately after spanking? ☐ Yes ☐ No

In this situation, did the child try to run to your spouse for comfort? If so, how did you and your spouse handle that?

Has your spouse *ever* corrected one of your children and that child ran to you for comfort? What did you do?

Did the child make restitution if necessary? ☐ Yes ☐ No

Have any of your children openly defied your authority or deliberately disobeyed a clear instruction lately? If so, which child?

Do you plan to stop the disobedience? ☐ Yes ☐ No If so, how?

If you were physically abused as a child, and there are still deep emotional pain and frustrations, seek professional help. A good professional counselor can help you gain the knowledge and strength to be sure you have a balance in your discipline. If your anger gets out of control when you are spanking, do not use this method of correction until there is healing and you are able to control your anger.

Methods 3 and 4: Natural and Logical Consequences

Would you like to learn a method of discipline . . .

. . . that is extremely effective and that changes children's behavior?

. . . that gives the parent a lot of control?

. . . that can replace spanking as the major method of correction as children leave the preschool ages and begin school?

. . . that will eliminate power struggles—especially from strong-willed children?

. . . that will develop responsibility in your children?

. . . that eliminates arguing and complaining?

. . . that is positive and builds a child's self-esteem?

Logical consequences is a method of discipline that will give parents all of the benefits listed above! With this method of discipline, you will also learn how to use a related method—natural consequences. *Natural consequences* is used much less often, but is extremely effective when you need to use it. We will start by explaining it.

I. Natural Consequences

Using natural consequences means that the parent stays out of the way and lets nature run its course.

Parents have a responsibility to shape and mold their child's will; however, some parents take *too* much responsibility for their children. At times children learn best when they experience the *results of their poor choices* (within limits, of course).

Here are some examples of how parents can use natural consequences:

Problem 1. Todd, age five, doesn't want to wear shoes to his swimming class. Mother knows he has to walk across the hot pavement in the parking lot and encourages him to wear his shoes, but Todd argues vehemently.

Solution using natural consequences. Mother allows Todd to go without shoes, but she does not rescue him from the situation. Todd runs as fast as he can and experiences the pain of a hot pavement on bare feet. He suffers the natural consequences of his choice. He wears shoes next time. (If he is strong-willed, he may experience the pain several times before putting on shoes, but he will eventually put shoes on if the pavement is hot enough.)

Problem 2. Jeff's responsibility is to feed his dog. Jeff loves his dog, but often forgets to feed the dog. (He knows Mom will do it if he doesn't, so why should he take the responsibility?)

Solution using natural consequences. Jeff forgets to feed his dog for 24 hours. Mom doesn't feed the dog either. Mom mentions to Jeff that his dog seems hungry. Jeff gets upset and feels sorry and responsible for his hungry dog. Jeff becomes more responsible to feed his dog because he knows the dog will go hungry otherwise. (If Jeff would not care for his dog, Mom would not let the dog go hungry, but would find another home for the dog where he would be cared for.)

Problem 3. It is cool outside and Michelle doesn't want to wear her sweater to school. She argues and fusses about not wanting to wear the sweater.

Solution using natural

consequences. Mom lets Michelle go to school without the sweater. Michelle is cold and gets goose bumps as she walks to school. All day she wishes she had her sweater. The next cool day Mom doesn't say anything; Michelle wears her sweater because she does not want to be cold all day.

Problem 4. Kathy, age eight, is forgetful. She forgets to take her lunch to school once or twice every week. Usually, Mom drives to school to deliver Kathy's lunch to her when she forgets.

Solution using natural consequences. Kathy forgets her lunch. Mom does not take her lunch to school. Kathy goes without lunch at school and gets hungry.

Letting children learn the natural consequences of some of their behaviors helps them to learn to be more responsible. *Children who are protected and don't learn that there are consequences to bad choices learn the hard way, when they are adults, that poor choices result in pain and suffering. Only, in adulthood, the pain is greater and there is more at stake.*

Of course, if there is real danger of harm to the child or someone else, do not use natural consequences.

II. Logical Consequences

In natural consequences there was a built-in consequence that naturally happened; the parent did not have to intervene, just allowed the child to experience the pain of his choice. But in logical consequences the consequence is built in by the parent. The parent intervenes and structures a plan of consequence that is not naturally there.

To use logical consequences, a parent plans a negative consequence for the child that is logically related to the misbehavior. For example, a child writes on the wall with a crayon. The logical consequence is that the child cleans the marks off the wall himself. The consequence is negative because it's no fun cleaning marks off a wall; it takes time and effort that could be spent playing. The consequence is related to the child's misbehavior because the marks wouldn't be there except the child put them there. The child sees a relationship between the consequence and his misbehavior.

There are a lot of advantages to using logical consequences. Here are a few:

1. When a parent uses logical consequences, he has a lot of control over the child's behavior, but uses it for the child's good.
2. It can be used with children of all ages, although it is most effective with children ages five and older (including teens).
3. It teaches children to be responsible.
4. It weakens the power struggle between the parent and child. This is especially helpful with strong-willed children.
5. It is a method of child discipline that gets results.
6. Logical consequences corrects misbehavior with very little talk —just action.

There is one problem, however. Developing logical consequences is a skill that takes practice. You *can* learn how to use logical consequences by doing the exercises and activities that follow.

Study the definition and the examples of logical consequences that follow. Remember that using logical consequences means . . .

A PARENT PLANS A NEGATIVE CONSEQUENCE FOR THE CHILD THAT IS LOGICALLY RELATED TO THE MISBEHAVIOR.

Problem 1: Bob was told to bring his bike in overnight and put it in the garage. Bob repeatedly left it outside.

Logical Consequence: If Bob leaves his bike outside overnight, he cannot have it for two days. The consequence is *negative* because Bob loves his bike and wants to play with it every day. The consequence is *logical* because, if Bob wants to play with his toys, he must learn to care for them.

Problem 2: Kelly, age ten, dresses slowly in the morning and doesn't care whether she is ready or not for school by her departure time of 7:30 a.m.

Logical Consequence: If Kelly is not ready for school by 7:30 a.m., she will have to go to bed 30 minutes early tonight so she has the energy to get ready in the morning. The consequence is *negative* because Kelly hates to go to bed early at night, and it is *logical* because more sleep will give her more energy in the morning.

Problem 3: Kurt stores his basketball in the living room because he plays with it a lot and the living room is near the door outside. He refuses to put it away in his room or in a special place in the garage.

Logical Consequence: If Kurt's basketball is not put away in his room or the garage, his mother will take it and put it away for a week. It is *negative* because Kurt's favorite pastime will be denied, and it is *logical* because Kurt has control over where he puts the ball. He has been given storage for all his toys in his room. He will learn to keep toys in the proper places if he wants to play with them.

Practice planning logical consequences. Read each of the following problems and write down a logical consequence for each one:

1. An eight-year-old child carelessly spills her milk.
   Logical Consequence:

2. A child makes his bed in the morning, but does it very sloppily. He has been taught how to make his bed and is capable of doing a neat job.

Logical consequence:

3. Danny, age six, walks through the kitchen tracking mud.
   Logical consequence:

4. A nine-year-old continually leaves his skateboard, sports magazines, and toys all over the family room.
   Logical consequence:

5. John, age ten, rides his bicycle down the middle of several streets in his neighborhood. He has been taught to ride near the curb on the right side of the street.
   Logical consequence:

6. Amy, age nine, is consistently late for dinner.
   Logical consequence:

7. A child walks in and out of the house and forgets to close the door.
   Logical consequence:

8. Mark, age four, loves to play and will not come inside when he needs to go to the bathroom. He usually waits too long and then wets his pants on the way inside.
   Logical consequence:

9. Kelly, age ten, dresses slowly in the morning and doesn't care whether she is ready for school by her departure time of 7:30 or not. (One logical consequence was given in the examples. Name one or two additional logical consequences to this situation.)
   Logical consequences:

(Turn to page 110 and check your answers.)

PRINCIPLES TO REMEMBER IN ORDER TO USE LOGICAL CONSEQUENCES EFFECTIVELY:

1. *If you are angry, you will not be able to use logical consequences effectively.*
2. *Communicate with the child first.* Always begin with communication whenever you use any method of correction. Tell the child the logical consequence that will take place if the misbehavior happens again.
3. *The consequence must be negative to the child.* What is negative to one child is not necessarily negative to another child. You need to know your child's likes and dislikes.
4. *The consequence must be logically related to the misbehavior.* In other words, there must be a relationship between what the child did and the consequence that the parent plans.
5. *The child must have the freedom to make his own choice.* Do not use logical consequences if you get mad if the child chooses the consequence; then you don't really want him to have a choice. A strong-willed child will test you to see if he *really* does have a choice. You cannot interfere with the child's decision making. Giving a child the freedom to "blow it" in these circumstances will teach him responsibility. It is better that he learn to be responsible now rather than in adulthood. If he does not have a certain amount of responsibility at three, at eight, or 15, he will not know how to handle responsibilities in his adult life.
6. *Stay out of the way and let the consequence do the correcting.* Let the child take the consequences of his action; do not rescue him. If you find that you are emotionally involved, think about the positive growth and responsible behavior that is developing in him.
7. *Be sure that the task involved is within the child's capabilities, and the consequences are reasonable.* He or she may be capable, but not experienced in doing the task. If so, lovingly teach the child how to do the task while he or she is doing it.

33

CASE STUDIES: Read each of the following case studies and then check the number of the principle(s) from above that were violated, if any.

CASE STUDY 1

Stevie loves to ride his bike in the street gutter, where there is a trickle of water. As he rides, the water from the gutter splashes up because there is no mudguard on his bike. The result is that there are spots of dirty water all over the back of his shirt every time he rides his bike in the gutter. After scrubbing the spots off of several shirts each week, Mom finally got mad one day and told him to get into the washroom. Mom made Stevie scrub all the spots from the dirty gutter water off of all of his shirts. After the third shirt, she told him to get out and she would do the rest because he was too slow.

Check the box for each principle that was violated:

☐ 1   ☐ 2   ☐ 3
☐ 4   ☐ 5   ☐ 6
☐ 7   ☐ None

CASE STUDY 2

Susie, age six, lives on a busy street, and her best friend lives across the street. They love to roller-skate together, but Susie's mother has told Susie that she is not to wear her roller skates while crossing the street because the street is too busy and dangerous. One morning Mother saw Susie roller-skating across the street and fall, as a car was coming down the road. Mother called Susie in and told her she would not be able to go outside for the rest of the day. Susie went into the family room, turned on the TV and enjoyed TV the rest of the day. Her friend came over to Susie's house, and they played together.

Which principle(s) was violated?

☐ 1   ☐ 2   ☐ 3
☐ 4   ☐ 5   ☐ 6
☐ 7   ☐ None

CASE STUDY 3

Sandy, age 17, shares a small bathroom with her two teenage sisters. Each sister has her own curlers, cosmetics, etc. If one of the sisters doesn't put her cosmetics away, there is little room for the next sister to have a place to put her things while she gets ready for the day. Sandy inevitably left her cosmetics all over the counter even after many reminders and much pleading.

Mom and Dad finally warned Sandy that if she left her cosmetics on the counter again, she would not see the cosmetics for a week. The first morning Sandy remembered to put her cosmetics away, but the second morning she left for school, and her cosmetics and curlers were spread over the counter. Mother picked up Sandy's things and put them away for one week. Sandy fussed, but her parents did not give in. After a week, they were returned to Sandy. Sandy was careful to put her things away from then on.

Which principle(s) was violated?

☐ 1   ☐ 2   ☐ 3
☐ 4   ☐ 5   ☐ 6
☐ 7   ☐ None

CASE STUDY 4

Amy, age four, is so loving and naive that she would go anywhere with anyone. Her family lives in an apartment and her parents felt it was important to make the rule that Amy must get permission before she goes into anyone's apartment. One day Amy met a new friend, Kim, and was invited to play in Kim's room. Amy went into Kim's apartment but did not get permission. Kim's parents were not home, only her older brother. When Amy's parents found out, they brought Amy home and told her that she would not be able to have any special treats for a month because she disobeyed them.

Which principle(s) was violated?

☐ 1   ☐ 2   ☐ 3
☐ 4   ☐ 5   ☐ 6
☐ 7   ☐ None

CASE 5

Mike is an extremely strong-willed child. In the early preschool years his parents tended to be very strict with him. As they grew in their parenting, they realized that he needed more freedom and a more positive environment with more choices. When he was four years old, they decided to begin using logical consequences. He then had a choice (1) to correct his misbehaviors or (2) to experience the negative consequences. Each time his parents gave him a logical consequence, he would continue the misbehavior and then take the consequence. He kept choosing just the opposite choice than they desired, just to see if he really did have a choice. This disturbed his parents, and they stopped the plan because they thought logical consequences would help him change his misbehavior.

Which principle(s) was violated?

☐ 1   ☐ 2   ☐ 3
☐ 4   ☐ 5   ☐ 6
☐ 7   ☐ None

(Check your responses to these case studies on page 110.)

III. Applying Natural and Logical Consequences in Your Home

1. List below all the frustrating problems that you are experiencing with your children at this time. List as many as possible.

2. As you look over your list above, decide whether a logical or a natural consequence would be effective for each problem. Write L or N beside each one.

3. Select one problem that can be solved by logical consequences and circle it.

   a. What is a logical consequence?

   b. Use communication first. Write the words that you will use to explain to your child the logical consequence.
   "If you (describe misbehavior) . . .

   Then (state logical consequence) . . ."

   c. Give the child the freedom to choose. Then, if necessary, enforce the logical consequence. Afterwards, write what your child's choice was and describe your enforcement of the logical consequence.

   d. Evaluation. Read over the "Principles to Remember in Order to Use Logical Consequences Effectively" on page 33. Did you follow all of those principles?
   ☐ Yes   ☐ No
   If not, which principle do you need to remember next time?

4. Look over your list of problems in #1. Is there a situation where natural consequences would be an effective method of discipline? Write that problem here:

   a. What is the natural consequence?

5. Future discipline problems. If your child is more than five years old, practice planning logical consequences for as many discipline problems as possible. Use the following plan:

   Step 1: Problem exists; child is misbehaving.
   Step 2: Brainstorm ideas for five minutes and see if you can come up with a logical consequence for this problem.
   Step 3: Use communication first. State to your child the logical consequence you *will take* (in the future) if the misbehavior happens again.
   Step 4: Allow the child the freedom to make his choice.
   Step 5: If child chooses to misbehave, take the action that you said you would and enforce the logical consequence.
   Step 6: Do not feel sorry for the child or get emotionally involved. You need to stay out of the way and let the consequence do the disciplining.

Method 5: Rewards

I. REWARDS AND LEVELS OF DISCIPLINE

Remember the three levels of discipline?

As you mold and shape your child's behavior, you will be constantly moving from one level to another. Rewards are effective if used on the level of *training,* rather than correction.

Training means helping a child form habits and develop proficiency in areas in which the child has been instructed. It is helping him develop positive *patterns* and *habits.*

The following are examples of training times when you can use rewards with children:

- being potty trained
- using proper manners
- completing homework assignments
- doing chores without being reminded
- washing his face at night

There are times when children know what their parents have instructed them to do and are able to do it, but just don't want to. At that time a child needs correction. If a parent offers a child a reward for correct behavior when the child is being rebellious and wanting his own way—that is bribery! Don't bribe children to be good. But when they need training, help them learn by providing rewards as motivators.

One area where it is sometimes unclear whether correction or training is needed is helping children to break bad habits. A habit is a behavior done unconsciously and without premeditation. Because habits are done unconsciously, they are difficult to break. Logical consequences is one way to help correct bad habits. A bad habit needs *retraining,* and rewards can also be used as strong, positive motivators.

List two specific times that you have used rewards with your children.

1.

2.

Behind each example write the words training or correction, depending on the level of discipline you were dealing with.

II. TYPES OF REWARDS

Basically, there are two types of rewards—intrinsic rewards and extrinsic rewards. An *intrinsic reward* exists within the child when he does what is good or right. When your child is able to follow your instructions, he has a good feeling about himself, a sense of accomplishment and satisfaction. Self-respect—is the best reward possible, and is more satisfying than extrinsic rewards.

However, parents can influence behavior positively and encourage intrinsic rewards by careful use of *extrinsic rewards.* These rewards are external: they come from outside the child, are given by others. Parents can give three kinds of extrinsic rewards:

1. *Social rewards* (most important type of extrinsic reward) includes words of praise, approval or appreciation; hugs and affection; attention; looks of approval; smiles; a kiss; a wink.
2. *Activities and special privileges* such as having a friend overnight; special time with Mother or Father; having a party or picnic; trip to a nearby park; getting to stay up later; going to a ball game or zoo; no work for a day; or any activity selected by child as a fun one for him.
3. *Tangible rewards* include ice-cream cone, gum or favorite food; cookies; chips; box of animal crackers; soda pop; toy, record, book or clothing child has been wanting; money.

Which types of extrinsic rewards have you used with your children so far?

Of the three types of extrinsic rewards that parents can give, the most important and lasting is social rewards. To be effective, though, social rewards must be sincere. They are not to be used to manipulate a child (this can easily be done with preschoolers)—they are to be sincere expressions of compliments and appreciation.

Parents need to emphasize social rewards and realize that they are the most important type of extrinsic reward that could be given to a child.

When using rewards, remember

the following principles:

1. Couple tangible rewards, special activities and privileges with social rewards.

2. Don't overuse rewards, giving out too many over long periods of time. Use them at times when the child is struggling to grow and needs encouragement and training to develop positive habits or patterns of behavior.

3. Select rewards based on the interests of the child. A reward to one person may not be a reward to another.

4. Give a variety of rewards. A reward can be overused and its effectiveness lost.

5. Do not give large rewards for small tasks. Select a reward that is compatible with the effort the child makes.

6. Use money as a reward as seldom as possible.

7. Don't reward for daily routine duties (see Project 14 on chores), but you can reward for duties that are done *without being reminded over a period of time*—day, week, or month, depending on the age of the child.

8. When you begin to give a reward for a particular good behavior, be extremely consistent and reward the behavior every time.

9. After a behavior is established give rewards intermittently.

III. HOW TO USE REWARDS WITH YOUR CHILDREN

You can apply the preceding material by working through a simple three-step plan for using rewards with your children.

Step 1   *Give social rewards*

liberally to your children.

Social rewards cost nothing and there is no limit to their supply. Use them often. The strongest rewards we can give our children are words of appreciation, approval, or praise.

Think of all the remarks you make to your family each day. How many of those remarks are positive remarks and how many are critical?

Circle where you feel you are right now . . .

Extremely critical with others	Extremely positive with others

1   2   3   4   5   6   7   8   9   10

Draw a square around the number you desire to be.

Sometimes parents see negatives in their children's lives more than they see the positives. How can one develop positive responses to others? Listen to what the Bible says:

"Finally, brethren, whatever is true, whatever is honorable, whatever is right, whatever is pure, whatever is lovely, whatever is of good repute, if there is any excellence and if anything worthy of praise, let your mind dwell on these things" (Phil. 4:8, NASB).

"For as he [a man] thinketh in his heart, so is he" (Prov. 23:7).

List each family member, then beside each one write something that is of good report, lovely, pure, right, honorable, etc.

Consider the child who is the most difficult for you to raise. Which child is it?_____

List three positive qualities that you see in that child's life now.

1.

2.

3.

Tell your children the positive qualities that you see in their lives. Also practice using positive phrases like:

An excellent job!
Good work!
You worked hard!
I'm proud of you.
Much better!
Very good.

What an improvement!
You did it!
I like that.

Even though our words are extremely powerful, there are other social rewards that are important to use. They include smiles, hugs, giving attention, looking interested, listening, looks of approval, etc.

If you did not receive these warm expressions of love when you were a child, it will be harder to give these to your children. You may need to consciously work at these goals of giving social rewards if they have not been modeled for you when you were young.

Step 2 *Select four changes in behavior that you desire for one of your children.*
1. *Select a child between 4 and 12 years of age for this project.*
   a. List four behaviors that you desire this child to have in column 1 of the chart below. Perhaps these are areas where you have instructed your child, but he is just learning and does not follow your instructions as a habit or pattern. For example, using proper table manners, completing his homework, not hitting when he is angry, being ready for school by a certain time each morning, etc. (Do not list chores. They will be handled differently on Project 16.) Write these behaviors in the chart before proceeding.
   b. In column 2 rewrite any behaviors that are stated in the negative. A child needs to know what he *should* do, not just what to stop doing. For example:

NEGATIVELY STATED—

Don't be late.

Don't hit your little brother.

Don't wet your pants.

POSITIVELY STATED—

Be on time.

Tell your little brother what you are angry about instead of hitting him.

Keep your pants dry all morning (day, week, etc.).

   c. Finally, in column 3 rewrite each of the behaviors being as *specific* as possible. In order for a child to comply with the behavior that you desire, it must be very clear to him. Children need specific details. For example: "Be on time for school" should be changed to "Be ready for school by 7:30 a.m." Giving a specific time gives more specific details.

SELECTING BEHAVIORS FOR REWARDS CHART		
1. Changes in behavior desired	2. Restated positively rather than negatively	3. Behavior in specific terms

2. *Reproduce the rewards chart on page 106 at the end of this book.* Select two *specific* behaviors from column 3 above. Each time your child accomplishes one of these behaviors, he will receive one point as indicated on the chart. If one behavior far surpasses the other in effort, either break it down into smaller steps, if possible, or give two points for that behavior. You may desire to fill in only one behavior and focus on changing.

3. *Decide on a reward for your child to earn* if *he accomplishes those behaviors.* Remember to select a reward based on your child's interests, not your interests. Explain that you are planning a fun way for him to work hard on some things that he is growing in, that it involves receiving a reward.

Ask your child to share with you some things that he would like to work for. If your child runs out of ideas, make some suggestions of tangible rewards, special activities and privileges. (Refer to page 36 for ideas.) List your child's desired rewards below:

Child 1 _____
Special activities & privileges

1.

2.

3.

Tangible rewards

1.

2.

3.

Child 2 _____
Special privileges & activities

1.

2.

3.

Tangible rewards

1.

SEARCH FOR TREASURE

NAME_____(50 POINTS)
_____ = 1 POINT
_____ = 1 POINT
ACTIVITY OR REWARD CHOSEN:_____

2.

3.

Then select one reward to use with this chart. Be sure it is not too large—just compatible with the effort he will be making to get 50 points. You might want to estimate the possible number of points per week to discern approximately how long it will take. Select a special privilege or activity as a reward first if there is one that would motivate him. Otherwise use a tangible reward that he has listed. The reward should not exceed $5 in value. See the accompanying sample rewards chart.

4. *Share this fun chart with your child.* Point out (a) the behaviors that he can work toward, (b) the point system for each behavior, (c) his goal = 50 points, and (d) his reward when the goal is reached. Discuss any details he has questions about, and be open to make minor adjustments, if needed.

5. *Post chart on the refrigerator or predominant place in your home.* Each time your child earns a point, ask him to darken one of the blanks around the border of the chart. Be consistent and reinforce your child *every* time that he does these behaviors.

6. *When your child completes the chart, give him his reward within 24 hours, if possible.* It is important to give rewards immediately. A child can be discouraged or disappointed if he has worked very hard for a reward and it is put off indefinitely.

7. *Remember to include social rewards* as you are giving out special privileges and tangible rewards.

8. *Don't overuse these charts.* Use the rewards chart with one child at a time. The rewards chart can be used with different children at different times. It is not to be used all the time with a child—just when you desire to build in certain habits and patterns of behavior.

Step 3 *Give your children*

unscheduled rewards using the coupons on page 107.

Surprise your child by rewarding good behavior, especially in areas where a child has put forth an effort or accomplished a desired behavior that you have been trying to teach him.

There is a set of reward coupons at the end of this book. Children will be delighted to receive them. These coupons can be used for (1) special privileges and activities or for (2)

tangible rewards. They give the child something concrete to remind him of his special, positive behavior and growth.

Below are some sample coupons.

Repeat Steps 1-3 whenever your children need encouragement and motivation in the training stage. Rewards will encourage your child if not overused and if given sincerely, without trying to manipulate children.

DINNER FOR TWO

TO_____

FOR_____

_____

You have earned dinner out with
☐ DAD ☐ MOM ☐ A FRIEND
You choose the restaurant

SPECIAL ACTIVITY AWARD

TO_____ FOR_____

_____

You have earned a special activity of your choice

DAY_____

ACTIVITY_____

SPECIAL FAMILY ACTIVITY NIGHT AWARD

TO_____

FOR_____

_____

On_____night you can choose a special activity for our family._____

_____

YOU'RE GREAT!!!

NAME

is awarded_____

_____

_____

because _____

_____ .

Selecting the Best Method of Discipline

I. Extinction As a Method of Discipline.

There is one additional method of discipline that you will learn in this project—extinction. No, we don't mean extinguishing *the child;* we mean extinguishing or eliminating the *child's misbehavior,* by ignoring it.

Extinction is the opposite of rewarding a behavior. There is no reward or reinforcement for the behavior at all—the child misbehaves, and the parent ignores it and doesn't give the child any attention for the misbehavior. Ignoring a behavior is, of course, many times *not* an effective method of discipline. But there *are* times when it can be extremely effective.

The method of extinction or ignoring can sometimes be used with temper tantrums. The parent can walk out of the room and not even look at the temper tantrum. Then the child has lost his audience.

Extinction or ignoring can also be used effectively when children interrupt you. When children interrupt you, if you reward them by giving them attention, they will continue to interrupt. It works! But if you ignore them, they will stop contending for your attention when you're busy because it won't work. Of course, you need to use communication first. You can say, "If I am talking to someone and you want me, just come and stand by me and within a minute I will see what you want. When you call me over and over, and try to tell me something by interrupting me, I will not pay any attention to you." Then do just that; be sure you attend to them within a minute, especially preschoolers.

If the misbehavior is a pattern, it will take several times of ignoring it before it will change. Expect to be tested.

II. Six Methods of Child Discipline.

When you are dealing with a specific misbehavior, it is important to select the *best* method of discipline to use in that particular situation. Let's learn how to do this by reviewing the methods of discipline that you have learned in the previous projects.

Read each definition and select the correct name of that method of correction from the chart below. Then write the name in the blank.

METHODS
OF
DISCIPLINE

Communication
Spanking
Logical consequences
Natural consequences
Rewards
Extinction

_____ 1. Staying out of the way and letting nature run its course.

_____ 2. Physical pain, applied appropriately.

_____ 3. Strengthening or reinforcing actions so that they are more likely to be repeated in the future.

_____ 4. Planning a negative consequence that is logically related to the misbehavior.

_____ 5. Not rewarding a negative behavior so that it will be eliminated.

_____ 6. A preventative method in which opinions or thoughts are exchanged. As information is shared each person understands the other.

III. Practice selecting methods for specific situations.

Read each of the following situations and decide which method of discipline would be best for this type of problem. Assume that communication is always used first. Before each situation write one of the following:

- Spanking
- Natural consequences
- Extinction/ignoring
- Logical consequences
- Reinforcement/rewards
- No correction necessary

_____ 1. A two-and-one-half-year-old child runs the other way when Mother calls her.

_____ 2. A fifth grader does not work up to his capacity in school; instead he works hurriedly and sloppily and receives low grades when he is capable of better grades.

_____ 3. A ten-year-old frequently forgets to take his lunch to school.

_____ 4. A child consistently has bad manners at the dinner table.

_____ 5. A seven-year-old is mean to the cat and teases him.

_____ 6. A teenager borrows the car and often returns home one hour past curfew.

_____ 7. An eight-year-old won't eat dinner. He has a very poor appetite and is a picky eater.

_____ 8. Six-year-old Mark makes his bed in the morning but doesn't always get the bedspread even with the floor across the bottom of the bed.

_____ 9. After five-year-old Amy is tucked in bed and the lights are turned off, she calls to her parents and tries to engage them in conversation.

_____ 10. A seven-year-old tells a lie.

_____ 11. A four-year-old is aggressive and hits other children when she gets angry at them.

_____ 12. A five-year-old rides his bike in a busy street which he knew was "off limits" for him.

_____ 13. A two-year-old gets mad because she can't have her way, and she hits Daddy. After being told to stop, she hits him again.

_____ 14. Dad taught 11-year-old Todd, his son, to mow the lawn. The second week that Todd mowed, he missed a strip right down the middle of the backyard.

_____ 15. A three-year-old is not cooperating with potty training.

_____ 16. A preschooler refuses to stay in his bed during the night and usually ends up sleeping in Mom and Dad's bed by morning.

_____ 17. A seven-year-old has a habit of biting his fingernails to the quick.

_____ 18. A 16-year-old throws her clothes around her room. She doesn't hang them up or put things in the hamper for the dirty wash. Mother gets tired of picking up after her.

_____ 19. Susie tattles on her brother just to get him in trouble whenever she can.

_____ 20. A nine-year-old doesn't remember to feed the dog each day.

When selecting the best method of discipline for your children, consider the following:

1. Every child is unique and what works on one child does not always work on another child. So _consider your child's individuality_ and unique responses in selecting a method of discipline.

2. Your goal is a change in behavior; _use whatever method will get a change in behavior._ If one method doesn't change the behavior, try another method until you find one that works.

3. _Do not discard a method as ineffective until you have thoroughly studied and applied it._

Sometimes parents think a method is failing to get results when they have not fully understood how to use it. Review the chapters on each of the methods of discipline if you need to. Once you understand each of these methods, you will have confidence that you can deal with misbehavior because you know several methods to select from and know that you _can_ change your child's behavior when you take action to do so.

IV. Applying these methods of discipline to current frustrating problems in your home.

Think of five frustrating disciplinary problems that you have experienced in the past or are now experiencing in your home. List these situations below. Write the child's name and age, and then state the child's behavior in one or two sentences. (Do not describe what you have done so far.)

Problem Situation 1
    Child _____ Age _____
Description of child's behavior:

    Method Chosen: _____

Problem Situation 2
    Child _____ Age _____
Description of child's behavior:

    Method Chosen: _____

Problem Situation 3
    Child _____ Age _____
Description of child's behavior:

    Method Chosen: _____

Problem Situation 4
    Child _____ Age _____
Description of child's behavior:

Problem Situation 5
    Child _____ Age _____
Description of child's behavior:

    Method Chosen: _____

Review each of the methods of discipline listed below and select one for each problem situation. Write the method that you chose in the blank provided.
    Communication
    Spanking
    Logical consequences
    Natural consequences
    Reinforcement/rewards
    Extinction/ignoring
What goals do you want to set for yourself in using any or all of the six methods of discipline in your home?

Consistency Through Enforcing Rules

I. What are the rules at your house?

This project will help you clarify your family rules and learn some basic principles for making effective rules. Begin by listing all of the rules that you have for your children—spoken and unspoken. Rules may include bedtime, eating, chores, playtime, homework, etc.

If you are doing this project with your spouse, do not look at each other's rules until both lists are completed.

1

2

3

4

5

6

7

8

9

II. General principles about rules

1. A rule is any demand by a parent on a child. There are two kinds of rules:

   (a) Long-term rules are enforced over and over again.

   (b) Short-term rules are spontaneous commands.

2. An effective rule is . . .

   (a) *Definable*—It is clearly and precisely stated in detail. It is well defined in the *child's* mind. Which rule is fully defined?

   ☐ Mark, I want you to take the trash out every Saturday.

   ☐ Mark, on Saturdays I want you to empty every wastebasket in the house (check each room for a wastebasket). Empty them in the outside trash cans. Then return the wastebaskets to their appropriate place in each room.

   (b) *Reasonable*—It is in line with the child's capabilities; he has the ability to do it. Which rule is reasonable?

   ☐ (To a four-year-old child) Make your bed each morning.

   ☐ (To a seven-year-old child) Make your bed each morning. I'll show you how. First, let's find the sheet and pull it towards the top . . .

   (c) *Enforced*—You make sure the child complies with the rule. Don't make rules unless you are going to enforce them. Enforce rules by:

   (1). Setting a time limit. Have a good happening after, if possible. For example, "Do your chores before you go out to play."

   (2). Make sure that the task is done. No matter how much the child stalls, pleads, argues, tries to break the rule, etc., cause him to comply with the rule.

3. Set a few rules that are important and be consistent in enforcing them. Don't have too many rules; it is difficult to enforce all of them and it is discouraging to a child.

If you enforce a rule one day but not the next, a child doesn't know what to expect and becomes confused. It creates insecurity in a child.

III. Evaluating your family rules

Continuing to work separate from your spouse, evaluate your family rules. Your spouse can use a separate piece of paper to answer these questions.

1. Look over your list of rules at the beginning of this project and circle one that needs to be rewritten so that it is clearer and more precise. Rewrite the rule here, making it definable and reasonable.

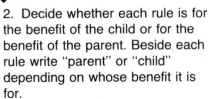

2. Decide whether each rule is for the benefit of the child or for the benefit of the parent. Beside each rule write "parent" or "child" depending on whose benefit it is for.

Are your rules mostly for your child's benefit or for yours?
- ☐ Mostly parent's benefit
- ☐ Mostly child's benefit
- ☐ They both equally benefit

3. Do your rules and expectations coincide with the capabilities of the age level of each of your children? If not, what changes do you need to make?

4. Is there any rule that may be discouraging for any of your children?

5. Is your tendency to have too many rules or not enough?

6. Write the date of the last time you enforced each rule beside each rule.

7. Cross out any rule that you are not willing to enforce. Then you will have fewer rules and can focus on being consistent with those rules.

8. Generally are your rules changing as your children grow and change?
☐ Yes ☐ No
If yes, give an example.

9. When was the last time that you had to change a rule?

10. In what areas are you frustrated now that you may need to change a rule or make a new one?

11. Share your list of rules and their evaluations with your spouse. Discuss together any changes that need to be made. Select one rule that you will focus on consistently enforcing during the next seven days, and write the rule below:

IV. When husbands and wives disagree about rules

A child needs both parents enforcing the rules in the same way or he will feel insecure.

God has created every person uniquely. Husband and wife have differing character traits and have been influenced by completely different childhood experiences. Therefore, it is normal and natural that they do not agree on all things.

However, differing opinions about child rearing can cause confusion for the children. Most disagreements about rules are not caused by concern about cruelty or serious permanent damage to the children; usually it is just a matter of opinion. It is important to have peace, harmony, and security in the home. The pain of conflict and disunity causes insecurity in children.

Read over your list of rules and copy down any rule which you enforce but your spouse does not (or vice versa).

Discuss the above rule with your spouse. Listen as your spouse shares how he or she feels about this rule; then share your ideas, feelings, and reasons for or against the rule. Together decide how to change the rule so that there can be consistency.

Thank God together for His consistency with you. Ask Him to help you be consistent with your children and to build consistency between you and your spouse.

Taking the "Chore" Out of Chores

Children love to play, but they don't always love to work! That is why getting children to do chores is sometimes a hassle.

But giving children responsibility in the home develops a sense of self-respect, teamwork, responsibility for themselves and others, and self-discipline.

It is best not to pay children for doing daily routine chores. Children who are paid for regular chores can begin feeling that they should be paid for everything they do and lose the concept of shared responsibility in the home.

However, when children do chores all week without being reminded and are very responsible, they should be rewarded for their consistency. A small, weekly reward will encourage children and give them an incentive to remember their chores.

A second list of chores, however, can be optional and involve pay. Children then will have an opportunity to earn money if they desire. Post the list of optional chores, with the amount you will pay, in a prominent spot.

This project consists of two simple, workable plans for chores for children. One plan is for preschoolers, the second is for children ages five and older.

I. Preschool Children. Children under age five learn about being responsible by learning to care for themselves and their toys and room. Look at the "Learning to Care for Myself—Chart" illustrated below. (At the end of this book is a copy of this chart to photocopy for home use.)

This is a weekly chart to help you encourage behaviors that you desire to see developed in your child. Preschoolers are learning how to care for themselves and their things more than actually doing chores around the house, so this weekly chart focuses on personal responsibilities.

To use this chart, list seven to ten behaviors that you would like from your preschooler each day. Be as specific as possible. Include personal hygiene, caring for possessions, and actions towards others in the family.

At the end of each day give your child a star or check for each behavior that he or she did. If your child has done all behaviors on the list or all but one, give your child a small reward at the end of that day just before bedtime.

When you begin this chart, you may need to require fewer behaviors to get the daily reward.

As the child is capable of doing more, make the requirement more. Later you can also add that the child do the behaviors without being reminded.

This chart may be used for several weeks. Use the chart again later when you see a need to build some new behaviors into your preschool child.

Remember to *emphasize social rewards* (praise, hugs, smiles, etc.) as well as tangible rewards for good behavior.

II. Chores for Older Children. This plan for chores involves two forms—"Daily Chores" and "Weekly Chores." Reproduce page 108 from the back of this book so that you can look at the forms while learning how to use them.

Checking up on a lot of chores

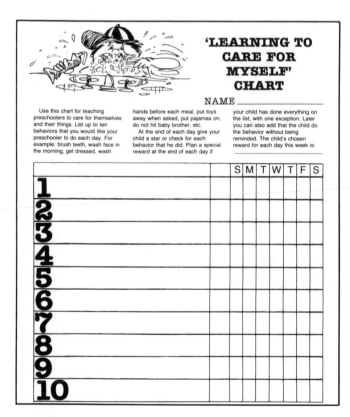

'LEARNING TO CARE FOR MYSELF' CHART

NAME_____

Use this chart for teaching preschoolers to care for themselves and their things. List up to ten behaviors that you would like your preschooler to do each day. For example: brush teeth, wash face in the morning, get dressed, wash hands before each meal, put toys away when asked, put pajamas on, do not hit baby brother, etc.

At the end of each day give your child a star or check for each behavior that he did. Plan a special reward at the end of each day if your child has done everything on the list, with one exception. Later you can also add that the child do the behavior without being reminded. The child's chosen reward for each day this week is:
_____

	S	M	T	W	T	F	S
1							
2							
3							
4							
5							
6							
7							
8							
9							
10							

with several children every day can be frustrating! A good plan is to divide chores into two categories: (1) chores that need to be done daily (setting the table, washing dishes, feeding the pet, making beds, etc.); and (2) chores that can be done once a week (vacuuming their rooms, dusting, emptying all the wastebaskets in the house, or whatever is a once-a-week job for your home).

Each child has his or her own set of daily chores, and each child also contributes when all family members work together for a period of time on weekly chores.

A. On the next page is a sample of the "Daily Chores" form. Use the "Daily Chores" form as follows:

1. Use one form per child.
2. Within the box is the list of chores that the child is to do daily. *Keep daily chores at a minimum!* Include only necessary things such as making beds, feeding pets, setting the table for dinner, washing the dishes, etc. This will eliminate a lot of frustration over follow-up of several children.
3. It is important that there is a time limit in which chores should be completed. A time limit is built into this form. Notice the word "Before" in the two large boxes. There are two times of the day that chores can be done, as the two boxes indicate. Usually one time is morning and the other is after school or after dinner. You can use other time variations that suit your family. A time limit is

set by filling in the words "before . . .," like "Before breakfast," or "Before play, after school," or "Before TV, after school," etc.

4. The child is to do all the chores by the time limit and then check off the list on the right-hand side of the chart.
5. When the time limit is up the parent can glance at the chart and see if the work is checked off.
   (a) If the chores are not checked off by the time limit, give the child an additional small chore of five to ten minutes. Circle the box that was not checked off on time.
   (b) If the child does his chores and also checks them off all week (with perhaps one exception), give the child a small reward for being consistent in his work all week. Be sure it is small (like a candy bar or special privilege) and not costly.
   Therefore, there is a negative consequence if the work is not done and a positive consequence if it is done consistently all week.

B. The second part of this chores plan involves weekly work and helps you as a parent to organize the heavier chores. On the next page is a sample of the "Weekly Chores" form. Use this "Weekly Chores" form by:

1. Having all the children do weekly chores together each week.
2. Weekly chores should ideally be

done at a regular time each week (like Saturday morning or Thursday evening). The children expect it and plan around it. The more children you have, and the more activities they are involved in, the greater will be the need to have a regular time.

3. As the children do their chores, the parent supervises. This gives you the time and opportunity to teach and train. To begin with, don't be a perfectionist. A lot of teaching may need to take place. Children naturally do not know all the steps involved in the chores they are assigned.
4. Weekly chores can involve Plan A—a list of tasks to be completed like cleaning own room, dusting, vacuuming all carpets, cleaning drawers in kitchen, etc.; or Plan B—a list of rooms to be cleaned. Use Plan A with younger children and until the children are older and trained to do most of the chores without supervision.
5. Set a time limit for weekly chores. It might be one hour or more. With younger children, plan a few minutes break during that time as needed.
6. If you have a child who really hates to work, emphasize to the child that one hour's work means one hour's *work*—not one hour's time. If the child plays or does not work during the time, add an additional five-ten minutes of work time for that child. This logical consequence needs to be stated only if a problem exists.
7. Checklists can be used when necessary to teach a child steps to a task. List all steps

involved in a task on a 3 X 5 card. Here are two sample checklists:

SETTING THE TABLE

1. Put tablecloth on table.
2. Place a plate, three utensils, and a glass for each person.
3. Place a napkin at each place setting.
4. Put salt, pepper, and butter on table.

CLEANING YOUR ROOM

1. Pick up all toys, clothing, etc., and put them away where they belong.
2. Vacuum the carpet (or sweep the floor).
3. Take all items off each piece of furniture, dust the furniture, then return items to their place.

8. Using the checklist, teach your children during the weekly work time. Follow this procedure:

(a) Do the task together several times, having the child do a few new steps each time.
(b) The child does the task alone.
(c) Praise the child's work; express appreciation.

Eventually, checklists can be eliminated. Checklists can be used for daily chores, also.

_____
NAME

_____
MONTH

Daily Chores

Before _____ A.M.	Before _____ P.M.
1.	1.
2.	2.
3.	3.

"Work hard and cheerfully at all you do, . . . remembering that it is the Lord Christ who is going to pay you. . . . He is the one you are really working for" (Col. 3:23, 24 TLB).

1st Week	1	2		3rd Week	1	2
M	☐	☐		M	☐	☐
T	☐	☐		T	☐	☐
W	☐	☐		W	☐	☐
Th	☐	☐		Th	☐	☐
F	☐	☐		F	☐	☐
S	☐	☐		S	☐	☐

2nd Week	1	2		4th Week	1	2
M	☐	☐		M	☐	☐
T	☐	☐		T	☐	☐
W	☐	☐		W	☐	☐
Th	☐	☐		Th	☐	☐
F	☐	☐		F	☐	☐
S	☐	☐		S	☐	☐

Chores completed and checked on time all week (except 1) = _____

Weekly Chores

Check one: Plan A ☐ List tasks to be completed. Plan B ☐ List rooms to be cleaned.	Person Responsible

---

48

How to Develop Self-Control in Your Child

The goal of discipline is *self*-discipline or *self*-control in the child. As a parent, your aim is to help your children develop their own inner controls.

A child's growth ideally should look like the chart at the bottom of this page.

The shaded area between the solid lines represents the amount of self-control a child should have. He has very little at birth and needs to grow each year into more and more self-control.

The area between the dotted lines represents the parents' control and influence. During the toddler years the parents need to exercise more control because the child has very little inner control. Each year as the child grows toward adulthood, he should be exercising *more* self-control. Parents should be exercising *less* parent control as the child grows in inner control.

The reason a parent corrects and sets limits on his child is so that the child will learn self-control and develop the ability to do the right thing when Mom and Dad are not around.

Parents need to begin very early developing self-control in their child because it is a process. It is not something that begins during the teenage years; it begins during the early preschool years.

Proverbs 25:28 describes a person who doesn't have self-control: "He that hath no rule over his own spirit is like a city that is broken down, and without walls." The word *rule* means control. So Scripture pictures a person who doesn't have self-control as a city that has no defense; it is helpless to defend itself against the enemies that come to take it.

One of the greatest gifts we can give our children is to set limits on them (lovingly, of course), to develop inner control, preparing them for the time when they are on their own to make their own decisions and choose their own values in life. A child who has developed self-control will find it easier to give himself to the goals he desires as an adult. He can also give himself to God because the child has control of himself to give himself to his Creator.

Write the name and age of your oldest child:

_____

List the areas that you want this child to be self-controlled or self-disciplined in when he or she leaves home early in adulthood (consider friendships, money, sex, job, relationships, selection of marriage partner, spiritual life, etc.).

1.

2.

3.

4.

5.

6.

7.

8.

9.

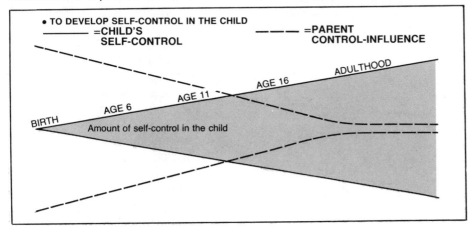

- TO DEVELOP SELF-CONTROL IN THE CHILD
——— =CHILD'S SELF-CONTROL   — — — =PARENT CONTROL-INFLUENCE

BIRTH AGE 6 AGE 11 AGE 16 ADULTHOOD
Amount of self-control in the child

49

10.

Next list the things that you can trust your child to do now even when you are not around. (Even a two-year-old can have self-control in specific areas.)

1.

2.

3.

4.

5.

In listing areas you want your child to have self-control in, you listed goals you have for your child. You have also analyzed where your child is now. There are many little steps that your child will have to make to go from where he is now to where you want him to be in adulthood.

Parents need to be working towards many little steps of inner control so that a child can reach the larger, more crucial goals that you have for them later in life. Look at the time you have with your children between now and when they leave home as opportunities to teach them and guide them and help them develop inner control so that they can do the right thing when they leave home.

What are some goals that you would like to have for your oldest child at this time to develop self-control in him or her now?

1.

2.

3.

Write the names of each of your other children over two years of age. Then identify two areas where each has developed self-control. (In other words, when you are not there, the child will do the right thing.)

Name: _____ Age: ___
Areas of self-control:
1.

2.

Name: _____ Age: ___
Areas of self-control:
1.

2.

I. How to develop self-control in your child.

The basic principle in developing self-control is:

Give your child as much freedom as he can handle responsibly.

There are several specific steps you can follow to develop inner control in your child. All the following steps are important; one *cannot* be emphasized over another principle or a child will not gain inner control.

1. *Set and enforce limits* on your child's behavior (and attitude as he gets older). A child who learns to live within the limits set by his parents learns that there *are* boundaries in life. Parents need to structure a child's environment so that the child is not allowed to do those things which he doesn't have self-control over. Setting limits in the preschool years lays a foundation for self-control all through life.
2. *Allow your child to make decisions and choices in less important matters.* Then a child will begin to learn the consequences of poor decisions.
   Someday our children will be on their own, making their own decisions entirely. If you as a parent allow them to make

decisions and value judgments in little matters when they are younger, then they will be more capable of making better decisions when they leave home.

3. *Use natural and logical consequences often during childhood.* These two methods of correction have a choice built into them. A child learns that his behavior can result in negative consequences for him. He will then learn to be more responsible so that he can avoid the negative consequence. (For further study on natural and logical consequences, review Project 10.)

4. *Give freedom with responsibility.* When a child asks for a freedom or when you think the child is ready, give your child freedom, but require that she be responsible with the freedom. If the child is responsible, continue to allow her to have the freedom.

5. *Restrict the child's freedom if he is not responsible.* But be positive and give him hope by saying: "We'll try again soon and see if you are ready to handle this freedom then."

Then after a few days, weeks, or months, whichever is appropriate, give the child the freedom again, stating that you think he can handle the freedom now. Be sure he knows what he needs to do to be responsible.

For example: to a three-year old . . .

"You may play in the front yard (freedom), but do not go into the street (responsibility)."

If the child goes into the street, you can say, "What was our rule about the street? . . . You may not play with your friends in the front yard the rest of the day . . . You'll need to play alone in the house or backyard for the rest of the day. We'll try again tomorrow and see if you can play in the front without going into the street."

Notice how the attitude of the parent is one of hope and love and belief in the child even though the child didn't have the self-control.

This pattern for giving children as much freedom as they can handle responsibly looks like the diagram below.

II. Evaluating self-control in your children.

How do you feel about the limits you set for each child?

First child: _____ Age: _____
Do you feel that you set . . .
☐ too many limits on this child?
☐ not enough limits?
☐ limits with a good balance of parents' decisions and child's decisions?

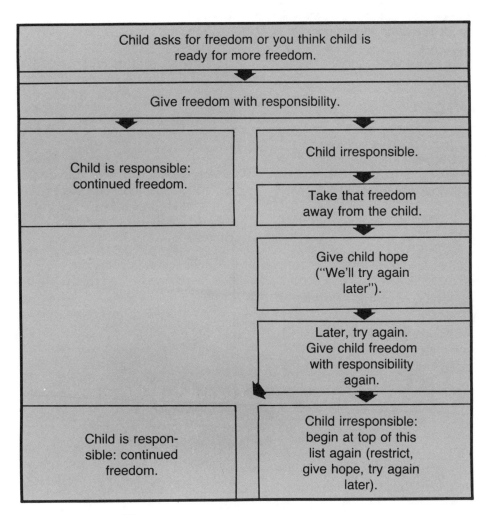

Child asks for freedom or you think child is ready for more freedom.

Give freedom with responsibility.

Child is responsible: continued freedom.

Child irresponsible.

Take that freedom away from the child.

Give child hope ("We'll try again later").

Later, try again. Give child freedom with responsibility again.

Child is responsible: continued freedom.

Child irresponsible: begin at top of this list again (restrict, give hope, try again later).

Second child: _____ Age: _____
Do you feel that you set . . .
- ☐ too many limits on this child?
- ☐ not enough limits?
- ☐ limits with a good balance of parents' decisions and child's decisions?

Third child: _____ Age: _____
Do you feel that you set . . .
- ☐ too many limits on this child?
- ☐ not enough limits?
- ☐ limits with a good balance of parents' decisions and child's decisions?

Describe the last time one of your children asked for more freedom in a particular area which he or she handled responsibly.

Describe a time recently when one of your children desired more freedom and you denied it. Why?

Did you give him hope that he could try again later?
- ☐ Yes. If yes, how?
- ☐ No. If no, why?

Did the child feel that you believed in him and was on his side?
- ☐ Yes   ☐ No
How do you know he felt that way?

Describe the last time a child was given freedom and wasn't responsible.

Did you . . .
- ☐ restrict the child from having that freedom for a while?
- ☐ let the child be irresponsible? If so, what did the child learn?

Describe the last time you used natural or logical consequences to correct a child over five. In what way did it help develop inner control?

Fill in the name and age of your oldest children below and circle the number that best indicates how much self-control they have *for their age.*

Name: _____ Age: __

1   2   3   4   5   6   7   8   9   10

No self-control	High amount of self-control

Name: _____ Age: __

1   2   3   4   5   6   7   8   9   10

No self-control	High amount of self-control

Circle the name of the child you feel is the most lacking in self-control.

Review the five principles of how to develop self-control in a child on page 51. Which principle(s) do you need to focus on in training this child?

Using these five principles, write your goals and plans for developing more self-control in this child.

Developing good self-esteem in your child is the *best* gift that you can give him or her. It is a gift that lasts a lifetime!

A child who feels capable and competent and has good self-esteem will have the resources to celebrate life with strength and creativity. This child will be a winner!

Self-esteem is established during the early years of life. It continues to grow during childhood. Parents are the greatest determining factor in whether a child has a positive self-image or a negative one.

What can parents do to build positive self-esteem in their children? The projects in this section focus on specific attitudes, skills, and behaviors that parents need in order to give their children the gift of good self-esteem

BUILD SELF-ESTEEM IN YOUR CHILD

Your Self-Esteem and How It Affects Your Child

I. Foundations of Self-Esteem

The first step to building your child's self-esteem is to build your own self-esteem. If your self-esteem is extremely low, it will be difficult, if not impossible, to build your child's self-esteem.

Maurice Wagner, in his excellent book *The Sensation of Being Someone,* defines self-esteem as a sense of being someone.

Some people have a sense of being someone. They value who they are. They have a realistic view of their strengths and weaknesses. They feel good about being themselves. They also feel that other people love and value them.

This mental picture that you have of yourself is called your self-image, self-esteem, or self-concept. A person may feel positive and good about himself . . . or he may dislike or even hate himself.

There are three dimensions of self-esteem as illustrated below:

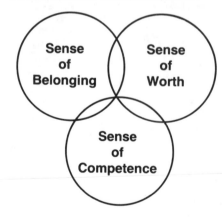

A *sense of belonging* means "having a sense of security and identity with others who love, accept, and support me."

A *sense of worth* means "being affirmed as a person of value; being cherished and respected."

A *sense of competence* means "gaining a sense of achievement; being affirmed as an able person."

So a person with positive self-esteem will have a sense of belonging, worth, and competence.[1]

Where does a person's self-image come from and how does it develop?

Norman Wright, in his book *Improving Your Self-Image,* answers this question by stating:

"The image we have of ourselves is built upon clusters of many memories. Very early in life we begin to form concepts and attitudes about ourselves, others, and the world. Our self-concept is actually a cluster of attitudes about ourselves—some favorable and some unfavorable. Our mind never forgets an experience. We may not be conscious of it, but it is still there."[2]

When you were a young child, you were very impressionable. The way the adults in your life treated you had a great influence on what you thought about yourself. Your parents were like mirrors, reflecting to you who you were. You believed their evaluation of you.

If your parents treated you with love and respect, if they cherished you, you drew the conclusion that you were important. But if your parents didn't cherish or respect you, you felt more like a "nobody." You placed less value on yourself—because those who cared for you didn't value you the way they should have.

You may have developed an extremely positive self-esteem as a child, or you may have developed an extremely negative self-esteem . . . or you may be anywhere in between.

What factors in your childhood

had a *positive* contribution to your self-image?

What factors in your childhood had a *negative* contribution to your self-image?

Which childhood influences affected your self-esteem the *most*—the positive or negative factors?

☐ positive influences
☐ negative influences

II. Evaluate Your Self-Esteem

Take the two short tests that follow and rate your self-esteem.

Test A. There are ten statements below all beginning with "I am . . ." Complete each of the statements with the first ten adjectives or descriptive words that come quickly to your mind to describe yourself.

1. I am _____ __

2. I am _____ __

3. I am _____ __

4. I am _____ —

5. I am _____ —

6. I am _____ —

7. I am _____ —

8. I am _____ —

9. I am _____ —

10. I am _____ —

Read over the above responses and put a + or − by each descriptive word, depending on whether the characteristic was positive or negative.

Then put a B, C, or W, before each numbered statement, depending on whether the descriptive word indicates a belonging, competence, or worth.

Test B. What is your self-image quotient?[3] Rate yourself below with the following scale:
  N - Never
  S - Sometimes
  U - Usually
  A - Always

____ 1. I handle crisis situations with relative ease.

____ 2. I rely on myself more than on other people.

____ 3. I am self-sufficient.

____ 4. I look to God as the primary and most reliant resource for help.

____ 5. I am secure and don't worry about the past or the future.

____ 6. I am affectionate and am not afraid to show my feelings.

____ 7. I can graciously accept a compliment.

____ 8. I refuse to feel sorry for myself.

____ 9. I believe that I, not God, am responsible for my inadequacies.

____10. I do what I think is right rather than what is expected of me.

____11. I stick to what I believe.

____12. I am sensitive to the unspoken, subtle needs of others.

____13. I like to do things for others.

____14. I am actively involved in doing what I consider to be worthwhile activities.

____15. I can find positives in negative situations.

____16. I can do almost anything if I put my mind to it.

____17. I can cope with frustrations in a positive way.

____18. I realize my self-worth.

____19. I have peace of mind.

____20. I accept others at face value.

Score this test by assigning a numerical value to each response as follows:
  Never 0
  Sometimes 1
  Usually 2
  Always 3

After assigning numerical values to the responses in the test, add up the total number of points you have in the test and write that number here _____.
Next find your rating on the scale below:

50-60   You may be fooling yourself, or bordering on a giant attack of ego.

35-50   You have a balanced, realistic sense of self-esteem.

25-35   You have about an equal amount of self-worth and insecurity but there is still room for improvement. You need to concentrate on enhancing your self-image in the areas where you scored lowest.

15-25   Your self-image definitely needs a boost. You need to isolate and reverse the negative patterns that are pulling you down.

0-15   You need to consistently use self-helps . . . and perhaps seek counsel from your pastor or someone you trust to help you eliminate your problems.

Now that you have begun to evaluate your self-image, the next step is to learn how to grow—wherever you are.

Your childhood is over, and you are now affecting someone else's feelings of competence, worth, and belonging—your child's. But you can only give away what you have.

As you grow in your self-image, you have added skills, abilities, and attitudes you can build into your child to help him have a positive self-image.

As you are more in touch with your feelings, you can help your child to be more in touch with his feelings.

As you are more assertive and able to express your needs, you can teach your child to be more assertive and express his needs.

As you learn what your special abilities and talents are and use them, you can teach your child to know his abilities and the joy of fulfillment as he exercises them.

As you learn better methods of communicating, you can teach your child to communicate in better ways.

As you interrelate with others and love them and have the sense of belonging that comes from friendships, you can teach your child the joy and rewards of loving others and being loved.

As you enjoy fellowship with your Heavenly Father and see life from a spiritual point of view, you teach your child that it is exciting to have a Heavenly Father who cares and watches over him.

As you love yourself, you have more capability to love others. That's why the Bible says, "Love others as you love yourself."

You can grow in your self-image. Here's how.

III. How to Improve Your Self-Esteem

In order to understand how to grow, we need to understand our Heavenly Father's role in our lives and His role in the development of our self-esteem.

A Christian has been accepted with an acceptance one will never find in the world—unconditional

acceptance from God, our Creator. The Trinity works in our lives to build our self-esteem in the following ways:[4]

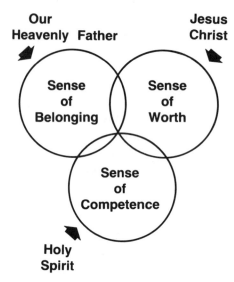

God, the Father, gives us a sense of belonging because we are part of His family. We belong to Him—He is our Creator. We also have a "family" sense because we feel kinship with others who have accepted Jesus Christ into their lives and become part of God's family. We also have a sense of belonging to Him because we will one day be with Him in mansions which He has prepared for us in Heaven (Jn. 14:2, 3).

Jesus Christ, the Son of God, has given us a sense of worth (having importance based on who we are, not on our performance) because He died for us even though we weren't righteous. Jesus totally accepts us—even in our state of sin—and gives us the gift of His righteousness. Jesus gives us a sense of worth because He humbled Himself to be limited to a body like we are and identified with us. He came in the flesh for us to know Him in a personal way

through salvation which He has provided for us.

The Holy Spirit gives us a sense of competence (being able) because He helps us to do the Father's work—not our own, but His. As we walk in His Spirit, there is a tremendous sense of being used by Him and being competent to represent Him through the guidance of the Holy Spirit. The Holy Spirit helps us develop a sense of competence by teaching us how to live and what to do moment by moment.

The single most important thing Christians can do to improve their self-esteem is to follow God's greatest commandment in Matthew 22:37,

> "Thou shalt love the Lord thy God with all thy heart, and with all thy soul, and with all thy mind."

"Loving God with our total self according to the first great commandment settles once and for all our search for self-identity. We know who we are: we are His, and we belong to Him. We know what we are: we are good and acceptable, for He has atoned for our sins. We know why we are: we have a good destiny, being created in His image and for His glory to live forever with Him."[5]

To love God with all our being is to love Him with all of our emotions and feelings, as well as our minds (our abilities to think and reflect and meditate on Him). He wants us to love Him totally.

Only God can give us unconditional love along with a sense of worth and competence. The world cannot offer unconditional love—sometimes we'll belong and sometimes we'll be alone in relationships in the world.

The world cannot offer us a sense of worth. We stand guilty before others and ourselves. We have a sin nature. But Jesus can wipe away that guilt and give us His righteousness. "There is therefore now no condemnation for those who are in Christ Jesus" (Rom. 8:1, NAS). The world cannot offer us a sense of competence. Being competent in worldly aspirations is not enough. Real competency comes when we live for God and share who He is daily with others. People are desperate for knowledge that God is not dead, but alive in His people. Our sense of competence comes when we witness to non-Christians and when we minister to and build up our sisters and brothers in Christ. We can be led daily by the Holy Spirit in both of these tasks.

IV. Personal Plans for Growth in Self-Esteem

Are you ready to grow and develop a more positive self-image? Here are some steps to follow:

A. *Accepting Jesus Christ as your personal Savior is the first step to building your self-esteem.*

Then you will really know who you are, your purpose in life, and your heritage. Have you accepted Jesus Christ as your personal Savior?   ☐ Yes   ☐ No
Read Romans 3:23; 6:23; 5:8 and John 3:36 and 1:12 in your Bible for further understanding.

B. *Guilt and Your Self-Image.*

Is there any sin in your life that is defeating you in your Christian walk? If so, name it.

Are you willing to confess and forsake that sin and then obey God in that area of your life?   ☐ Yes   ☐ No
Write a prayer to God about your responses to the preceding two questions.

For further reading about how guilt affects our lives read *Freedom from Guilt* by Bruce Narramore and Bill Counts (Santa Ana, Cal.: Vision House, 1974).

C. *Your Daily Quiet Time and Your Self-Esteem.*

A "quiet time" is a special time in the day that you spend with your Heavenly Father—talking to Him and studying His Word, the Bible.

As you fill your mind with the Word each day, you will be reprogramming your mind with God's values—not worldly ones. The Bible will strengthen you,

instruct you, guide you, and convict you. Your life can change *daily* as you obey God.

How many times last week did you have a quiet time? (Circle one.)
1   2   3   4   5   6   7

What is your plan when you come for a quiet time with your Father?
1. How often do you have a quiet time?

2. Where do you have your quiet time?

3. Number of minutes you usually take each day: _____

4. What is your plan for use of that time?

What changes do you desire to make in your plan for a quiet time?

If you don't have a plan for a daily quiet time, try this one:
1. *Relax*—Focus on the Lord and dispel all worries and concerns that are in your mind. Leave the world and be with Him for a while.
2. *Pray*—Keep a monthly prayer list and use it to remind you of things you want to pray about. At the beginning of

each month, write a new list.

3. *Meditate*—Meditate on a passage of Scripture. Select a book in the Bible and read through it. Read just a few paragraphs, then reread the passage two more times, slowly. Look for something in that passage that you can apply to your life. (Besides book studies, you can also study topics, Bible characters, etc.)

4. *Daily Spiritual Diary*—Each day add an entry to your "Spiritual Diary." Jot down the passage that you studied that day. Use your diary to write any of the following: how you plan to apply the Bible passage, what you learned, how you are feeling that day, your special prayers to the Lord for that day, and struggles you are having. Keep your diary intensely personal.

Select or adapt one of the following time plans . . .

Plan 1—*15 minutes* a day
Relax.............................. 1 min.
Pray................................ 3 min.
Meditate on the Word ...... 8 min.
Daily Spiritual Diary .... 3 min.

Plan 2—*30 minutes* a day
Relax.............................. 1 min.
Pray................................ 6 min.
Meditate on the Word .... 18 min.
Daily Spiritual Diary .... 5 min.

Write a prayer to your Father about any changes you would like to make in your quiet time. Tell Him specifically what you will promise to do in this area of your Christian life for the next week. Make a commitment for only a week and make realistic goals so that at the end of a week you have fulfilled your promise and know that you *can* make changes in this part of your life.

D. *Honesty and Openess in Your Relationships.*

On a scale of one to ten, how easily do you share yourself, your thoughts, ideas, and feelings with others? (Circle one.)

Closed—do not share easily   Extremely open with others

1 2 3 4 5 6 7 8 9 10

As you feel safe and secure in friendships, you will be more open to share yourself with others.

Make a list of your friends:

After each name listed above, write one of the following codes to indicate that person's level of friendship with you:

Ca = casual friendship
Cl = close friendship
I = intimate friendship

Intimate friends—those with whom we can share our most intimate thoughts, feelings, and ideas—are important in life. If you do not have an intimate friend, who do you know that you would like to develop a closer friendship with?

What can you do to reach out and show friendship to that person in the next seven days?

Proverbs 27:19 says, "As in water face reflects face, So the heart of man reflects man" (NASB).

This verse indicates that friends help us know ourselves better because they reflect to us who we are and we reflect to them who they are. So intimate friends are important in growing to know yourself and loving others.

If you desire further reading about friendships read *Why Be Lonely,* by Ford and Zorn (Niles, Ill.: Argus Communications, 1975), or *The Friendship Factor,* by Alan McGinnis (Minneapolis: Augsburg Publishing House, 1979).

E. *Work Towards Eliminating Negative Tendencies in Your Life.*

In your opinion, what negative tendencies do you struggle with in your life?

- ☐ worry
- ☐ anxiety
- ☐ fear
- ☐ depression
- ☐ perfectionism
- ☐ anger
- ☐ guilt
- ☐ critical spirit
- ☐ bitterness
- ☐ lack of self-control
- ☐ self-hate
- ☐ work too much
- ☐ Other: _____
- ☐ Other: _____

Read this list to your spouse and/or intimate friend. Ask them to give their opinions about areas you may be struggling with. Place a star by those areas.

As you look over the list of negative tendencies above, what is one area that you desire to eliminate from your life?

Find resources at your local Christian bookstore on this area and begin learning how to cope with this negative tendency and begin eliminating it from your life.

Of all the ideas in this section with plans for personal growth, select one area to begin with and check it below.

A. ☐ Knowing Christ as your personal Savior.
B. ☐ Dealing with guilt.
C. ☐ Maintaining a quiet time each day.
D. ☐ Establishing more or a deeper level of friendships.
E. ☐ Eliminating negative tendencies in your life.

Trying to accomplish all the goals you have explored in this chapter is unrealistic. Begin with just *one* area to work on—the one that you checked above. Write a prayer to God about that area and what you want to do during the next seven days in that area.

Select other ideas from this chapter as you have opportunity.

After you have worked through some of these areas, you can work further on developing a positive self-image by reading:

Improving Your Self-Image, by Norm Wright (Irvine, Calif.: Harvest House, 1977).

Put It All Together, by Maurice E. Wagner (Grand Rapids, Mich.: Zondervan Publishing House, 1974).

The Sensation of Being Someone, by Maurice E. Wagner (Grand Rapids, Mich.: Zondervan Publishing House, 1975).

You're Someone Special, by Bruce Narramore (Grand Rapids, Mich.: Zondervan Publishing House, 1978).

Your Inner Child of the Past, by W. Hugh Missildine (New York: Simon and Schuster, 1963).

Building Your Child's Self-Esteem

I. Your Child's Self-Esteem.

A child who has a good self-image, has a sense of being "somebody." Like anyone else who has a positive self-image, he values who he is. He has a realistic view of his strengths and weaknesses. He feels good about being himself. He also feels that other people love and value him.

A child who has a poor self-image will feel like a "nobody." A child with a poor self-image may dislike or even hate himself. He may not have a sense of belonging in his home, his classroom, in his neighborhood, or with his friends. He may be lacking a sense of being capable. He will be hesitant to try new things, fear failure, or be anxious when he is in new situations. He may be lacking self-worth, not feeling that he is important or worthy to be loved.

A child's self-image is a child's own view of himself. Parents who want to know how their child feels about himself need to ask the child—not assume that they know. *Within* the child is the key to his self-esteem.

The following two lists give some characteristics of children with positive self-images and children with negative self-images. Evaluate the self-esteem of each of your children as you read over these two lists.

A CHILD WHO HAS A POSITIVE SELF-IMAGE . . .

. . . is a happy child
. . . feels that he is liked by his peers
. . . is able to make friends
. . . is able to tell you some things that he is good at
. . . feels strong and capable

. . . feels secure in his home
. . . feels like an important person
. . . is able to give of himself to others
. . . feels good that he is doing his best in school
. . . does not measure his importance by grades and accomplishments
. . . feels like an important member of his family
. . . accepts his physical appearance and generally likes the way he looks
. . . attempts new tasks with courage
. . . tends to be creative in his own special ways
. . . shows love and kindness to others
. . . participates in games with other children rather than watching the majority of the time
. . . feels accepted for his uniqueness.

A CHILD WHO HAS A NEGATIVE SELF-IMAGE . . .

. . . may be unhappy much of the time
. . . may cry, whine, or withdraw
. . . may not feel liked by his peers
. . . may find it difficult to make friends
. . . may feel that he has to compete at home for attention
. . . may feel that he is in trouble much of the time
. . . may not know his own special abilities or talents
. . . may have lots of conflicts with peers or adults
. . . may not feel like an important member of his family
. . . may not attempt new tasks because he fears failure
. . . may feel he is only important if he performs well

. . . does not show love and kindness to others
. . . may watch other children playing but won't participate
. . . may be extremely competitive with other children
. . . is often mean to other children
. . . may feel that he is a disappointment to others
. . . may be afraid to volunteer answers in a group situation
. . . may be extremely shy
. . . may worry a lot

Parents have the greatest influence on a child's self-esteem. Parents are like mirrors, reflecting to their children how they see them. Statements like these are positive reflections to children:

"You can do it!"

"What a good helper you are, Suzie!"

"The new dress you picked out is beautiful—you have good taste."

"You are very responsible."

"Thank you for helping in our family and doing your part."

Statements like these are negative reflections to children . . .

"Be careful—I'm so afraid that you will hurt yourself."

"Can't you ever do anything right!"

"This is a sloppy mess—you'll never learn."

"Can't you act right??!"

"I've had it with you!"

Children are extremely impressionable. Children are also very trusting. They believe whatever their parents tell them. So when parents reflect positive character traits, strengths, or abilities that they see in their children, the children believe that they possess these things.

However, when parents tell or act as though their children are

When parents reflect . . .   children believe . . .

In contrast, when parents reflect . . .   children believe . . .

incapable, irresponsible, or not important enough to spend quality time with, children *believe* the negatives that are reflected.

Of course, we need to be realistic about children's developmental tasks and what they are capable of doing. However, many times children are ready and able to do *many* things that we may still want to hold the controls of.

As we learned in the previous chapter, the three dimensions of self-esteem—a sense of belonging, competence, and worth—are separate, but also very interrelated. Each project in this section will deal with building self-esteem in either one or more of these dimensions.

II. Respecting your child.

The foundation for building self-esteem in your child begins with respect. Though childish and immature, children are people—with feelings just like we have. Children need to be respected.

Respect means to consider worthy of high regard; to esteem. Every child is an individual with unique talents, temperament, and personality. It is fascinating to explore what a child thinks and feels on many subjects. Children

are good thinkers and delightfully fresh in their approach to life.

A child who is respected will open up and share with you who he is. There are many areas in which a child needs respect.

1. **Respect your child's feelings.**
Don't deny or ignore your child's negative feelings. If your child is mad, say, "You sure sound angry," and he will open up and tell you more. Admitting anger is the first step to dealing with it. Denial of anger prevents a person from dealing with it and resolving it. Besides listening to negative

feelings (like anger), be sensitive to your child's readiness to deal with it. When you are angry, sometimes it takes a while to calm down. The same is true with children.

2. Respect your child's unique qualities.

a) *Study your children and discover and appreciate their differences.*

Make a list of the positive qualities and character traits that each of your children possess. Then verbalize to each child how much you appreciate his character traits. Give them the feeling that one child could never take the place of another child, and that there are special things that you see in each one of them.

b) *Respect your child's unique qualities that are different from yours.*

You usually hear that your children are "just like you." But they all have differences from you that are sometimes difficult to accept. You may like peace and quiet and have a child with an extremely high activity level—a little one who runs circles around you while you are shopping. Or, Dad, you may love sports and have a son who has no interest in sports. It is extremely important to accept where your son or daughter is different than you! Differences in others is one of the great joys in life that help us broaden our world and perspectives on life.

c) *Respect your child's likes and dislikes.*

Allow your child many decisions in life that have to do with personal preferences. Let your children choose their clothes and decorate their rooms. Let them sometimes

choose what they want for dinner. If they absolutely hate some particular type of food, don't require that they eat that one food. (Don't you also have something that you think just tastes terrible?) If you have a strong-willed child, give him choices that involve personal preferences rather than moral issues of right and wrong. Strong-willed children want to feel that they have some control over their lives, and being able to have personal preferences really builds their self-esteem and confidence. Allowing a child his personal preferences says, "I love you and your uniqueness."

3. Respect your child's ideas and opinions.

Children have fascinating ideas. A child's mind is not clouded, like adults' minds sometimes are, trying to hide true feelings. Instead, children will tell you exactly what they think and why. Their ideas need to be listened to and respected. That does not mean you have to agree with them. If you want your children to feel free to tell you what is going on in their lives while they are away from you it is important to be open to your children's opinions when they are with you.

When your children are teenagers, they are more likely to tell you their opinions if they could tell you their opinions when they were children.

4. Respect your child's ability to think and solve problems.

Don't always solve problems for your children. They become good decision makers by making decisions and then living with the consequences. Allow your children to think through the pros and cons

in some more minor decisions in life, and then let them make the decision. Even when disciplining them, as they get into school-age years, sometimes say, "We need to solve this problem. What do you suggest that we do to solve it?" At times children will think of consequences and solutions that you would never think of—and ones that work!

If you have a child who is very compliant and who does not like to make decisions, refuse to make decisions which have to do with the child's personal preference; force the child to make his own decisions. Thus you prepare him for the adult world.

5. Respect your child during times you need to discipline him.

As studied in Sections 1 and 2, children need to be corrected. However, when you correct them, it is imperative that you respect them as people. Children need loving correction. If you are angry with your children while correcting them, you offend them. You are then involved in your own needs more than theirs. Review proper procedures for disciplining without anger in Project 4.

III. Test Yourself: How Much Do You Respect Your Children?

Select one of your children to evaluate. Select a child that is over three years old and one who either (1) has a temperament which is different from yours or (2) with whom you seem to have the most conflict. Read each question and check your response to that question.

Child selected: _____

DO YOU RESPECT YOUR CHILD'S FEELINGS?

	ALWAYS	OFTEN	SOMETIMES	RARELY	NEVER
1. Are you too busy to deal with your child's underlying feelings?	☐	☐	☐	☐	☐
2. Are you as polite to your child as you are with other adults?	☐	☐	☐	☐	☐
3. Do you give your child the right to some privacy when he is angry or discouraged?	☐	☐	☐	☐	☐
4. Do you ask for your child's forgiveness when you are wrong?	☐	☐	☐	☐	☐
5. When you make promises, are they only ones which you can and do keep?	☐	☐	☐	☐	☐
6. When your child is afraid or anxious, do you take time to talk with him and do what you can to dispel his fear or anxiety?	☐	☐	☐	☐	☐
7. Do you try to cheer up your child when he is sad?	☐	☐	☐	☐	☐
8. Are you impatient with your child?	☐	☐	☐	☐	☐
9. Do you lie to your children?	☐	☐	☐	☐	☐
10. Do you give your child the freedom to go to his room and shut the door to other family members if he wants to?	☐	☐	☐	☐	☐
11. Are you as careful in fulfilling your child's needs as you are in getting your own needs met?	☐	☐	☐	☐	☐
12. Do you force your children to share their special toys with other siblings or friends?	☐	☐	☐	☐	☐
13. Do you share your needs and feelings with your child at times when he is affected by them?	☐	☐	☐	☐	☐
14. Do you take disciplinary action when this child is being teased by another sibling?	☐	☐	☐	☐	☐
15. When your child is angry, do you listen to what is causing the anger?	☐	☐	☐	☐	☐
16. When your child is happy and excited, do you listen and share in his excitement?	☐	☐	☐	☐	☐
17. If your child has a high energy level, do you help him find activities and toys that are in line with his energy level?	☐	☐	☐	☐	☐
18. Do you support your child when he is hurt emotionally?	☐	☐	☐	☐	☐

DO YOU RESPECT YOUR CHILD'S INDIVIDUALITY?

	ALWAYS	OFTEN	SOMETIMES	RARELY	NEVER
1. Do you treat this child fairly, without favoritism to others?	☐	☐	☐	☐	☐
2. Do you accept your child's differences from your temperament and personality?	☐	☐	☐	☐	☐

	ALWAYS	OFTEN	SOMETIMES	RARELY	NEVER
3. Do you accept the abilities your child has that are different from yours?	☐	☐	☐	☐	☐
4. Do you let your child select his own clothing and shoes?	☐	☐	☐	☐	☐
5. Do you encourage your child in new activities if he desires to try them?	☐	☐	☐	☐	☐
6. Do you allow your child to learn skills that you never had an interest in?	☐	☐	☐	☐	☐
7. Do you tell your child stories about how hard your childhood was in order to minimize his problems?	☐	☐	☐	☐	☐
8. Do you serve your child food regardless of his preferences and then require that he eat all the food on his plate?	☐	☐	☐	☐	☐
9. When you are in a restaurant, do you let your child select his food within reason?	☐	☐	☐	☐	☐
10. Do you share with your child unique positive qualities that he possesses?	☐	☐	☐	☐	☐

DO YOU RESPECT YOUR CHILD'S IDEAS AND OPINIONS?

	ALWAYS	OFTEN	SOMETIMES	RARELY	NEVER
1. Do you ask your child for his opinion in casual conversations?	☐	☐	☐	☐	☐
2. Do you really listen when your child talks to you?	☐	☐	☐	☐	☐
3. Do you lack sensitivity to problems your child deals with in *his* world?	☐	☐	☐	☐	☐
4. Do you let your child ramble on while your thoughts are elsewhere?	☐	☐	☐	☐	☐
5. Does your child feel free to express an opinion that is contrary to yours?	☐	☐	☐	☐	☐
6. When you disagree with your child's opinion, do you make it look like your opinion is better than his because you are older and his parent?	☐	☐	☐	☐	☐
7. When someone asks your child a question, do you answer for him?	☐	☐	☐	☐	☐
8. Is your child free to tell you things about his world and his friends that he knows are contrary to your values?	☐	☐	☐	☐	☐
9. If your child shares something with you and asks you to keep it a secret, do you?	☐	☐	☐	☐	☐
10. Do you know your child's major concerns?	☐	☐	☐	☐	☐

	ALWAYS	OFTEN	SOMETIMES	RARELY	NEVER

DO YOU RESPECT YOUR CHILD'S ABILITY TO THINK AND SOLVE PROBLEMS?

	ALWAYS	OFTEN	SOMETIMES	RARELY	NEVER
1. Do you let your child make his own decisions when there is not a right or wrong answer in the issue—when it's a matter of preference?	☐	☐	☐	☐	☐
2. As your child gets older, are you giving him more freedom?	☐	☐	☐	☐	☐
3. Do you make almost all of the decisions in your child's life?	☐	☐	☐	☐	☐
4. Within reason, do you allow your child to suffer the consequences of poor decisions?	☐	☐	☐	☐	☐
5. If your child is complacent and wants you to make his decisions, do you force him into decision making?	☐	☐	☐	☐	☐
6. Are you overprotective of your child?	☐	☐	☐	☐	☐
7. Do you respect and support the decisions your child makes?	☐	☐	☐	☐	☐

Did you discover any areas where you would like to show more respect to your child? If so, describe the changes that you desire to make.

What Are You Reflecting to Your Children?

I. What are you reflecting to your children?

Select *one* child for this project—the child you are finding more difficult to raise right now. Keep this book near you throughout the next 24 hours and record as much interaction with this child as you can.

Use a separate piece of paper for additional space.

Child: _____   Date: _____

(Leave blank.)			YOUR WORDS TO CHILD: (Write one sentence per line.)
1	2	3	
			(Continue on a separate piece of paper, writing one sentence per line.)

In front of your recorded sentences are three columns which will be used for evaluation.

A. Using Column 1, mark as many statements as you can with the following code:
+ *Positive statements*—phrases or sentences that show acceptance, approval, affirmation, honor, respect, favor, or admiration.
− *Negative statements*—phrases or sentences that show disapproval, displeasure, criticism, impoliteness, disrespect, disregard, or disappointment.

You do not need to mark every statement; just the ones that are definitely positive or negative.

Number of positive statements:_____

Number of negative statements:_____

B. In Column 2 evaluate whether you reflect to your child that he is capable or not capable. Use the following code:
C "You are capable" statements from parent to child. Capable means having ability, being competent, qualified, or able.
NC "You are not capable" statements. Incapable means needing help, incompetent, unqualified, lacking in ability.

Number of "You are capable" statements: _____

Number of "You are not capable" statements:_____

C. How much of your talk focuses on correcting negative behavior and how much focuses on praising and encouraging positive behavior? Use

Column 3 and mark it as follows:
N Remarks that focus on negative behavior (correcting, criticizing, commanding).

P Remarks that focus on positive behavior (praising, encouraging, pointing out good behavior).

Number of statements focusing on negative behavior:_____
Number of statements focusing on positive behavior:_____

Look at the numbers that you recorded in each of the boxes above. What have you learned from this exercise?

Every parent reflects to his child his view of that child. When parents reflect negatives, the child believes the negatives. When parents reflect positives, the child believes the positives. It works like this:

Parent reflects negatives . . .

You hurt Jeff! Dont you know he has feelings? You are a terrible friend.

Child believes negatives . . .

Parent reflects positives . . .

Jeff is really sad right now. I know you can learn to be a good friend. What can you do to help the situation now?

Child believes positives . . .

What you reflect to your children is extremely powerful in influencing what they believe about themselves. The more you see and reflect positive character traits and abilities to your child, the more he will believe in himself and his abilities.

Take some time to look over your negative statements from your child's point of view. As you look at your negative statements in Column 1, pretend that each negative statement is being said to you. Think about what kind of feelings you would have if you were told these statements.

As you read the "not capable" statements in Column 2 remember that children **believe** what you say about them. When you feel that they are not capable, they believe they are not capable and then act out what they believe. In what areas are you telling your children that they are not capable? Can you change those "you are not capable" statements into more positive statements?

Finally, read over the statements in Column 3 focusing on the negative behavior, especially critical, fault-finding, or condemning remarks. Pretend someone is saying these negative statements to you. How would you feel? If you were a child, would you be discouraged by these remarks? Are there an equal number of remarks praising and encouraging positive behavior? How would you feel if you were a child and these positive remarks were said to you?

Why do parents give negative reflections to their children?	How to get out of negative reflections:
1. Generally, parents learned from their parents how to be negative. People usually parent the way their parents parented, or they take the opposite viewpoint as a reverse reaction to that style of parenting.	Learn new skills to change negative reflections into positive ones. This project focuses on how to get out of negative reflections. The next project will teach you specific skills that will help you get into giving positive reflections.
2. Sometimes, parents are frustrated and irritated with other problems, unrelated to their children. Even though they are disturbed by other problems, they take their anger out on the children.	A parent needs to get help for the problems that are frustrating him through . . . a) Talking the problem over with an intimate friend and seeking his advice. b) Using self-help books which apply to the specific problem. c) Seeking professional counseling when you cannot work it out yourself. Also, explain to the child that you are uptight and on edge because of adult problems. Verbalize to the child that you are not angry with him.
3. Parents do not take action to discipline their children and then get frustrated as they "put up" with the child's obnoxious behavior. Children usually get worse when they are not corrected for misbehavior because they feel insecure. They do not get their needs for security met when limits are not set. Because the parents don't take the responsibility to correct their children, the children are not a "delight" but a burden.	It is crucial to practice the concepts taught in Section II, "Ways to Discipline Your Child." You can enlist a friend or small group of friends to work through the projects at the same time you work through them. Then you will have friends to discuss the content with as well as the application. You will help each other learn. Seek counseling, if needed.

II. You can build your child's self-esteem by changing negative reflections into positive reflections.

A. Why do parents give negative reflections to their children and how can parents get out of giving negative reflections? Study the chart on the previous page to find the answers to these two crucial questions.

B. You can avoid giving negative reflections to your child by applying the following principles:

1. State your needs to your child.

As one human being related to another, you will find your child responding positively to statements of your needs. For example, "I need to work right now; we will talk about that as soon as I am done," or "I need to give your baby brother a bath right now. I cannot leave him alone in the bathroom. I know it is really frustrating when you cannot get your dresser drawer open. I will be there in about five minutes."

2. When you are frustrated or angry with other problems, be honest with your child and tell him how you are feeling.
   a) Identify the feeling.
   b) State the general cause. (You do not need to give details.)
   c) Describe your needs at the present time.

For example, you can say, "I'm upset with something right now. It has nothing to do with you. It is an adult problem. I need you to play quietly this afternoon." Then, if you need to, take action to help the child obey you, such as making plans for quiet activities.

3. Don't just talk to your child about his misbehavior, do something.

Some parents try to be patient even with behavior that desperately needs correction. But ultimately the parent gets angry and uses critical or sarcastic words which destroy the child's self-esteem. Children need to be corrected at the first appropriate moment.

4. Have realistic expectations of your child.

Know what your child is capable of. Realize that he is a learner and needs to be taught; the first level of discipline is instruction. Do not expect him to have table manners if you have not taken the time to teach him and then help him as he learns. Do not expect him to clean the bathroom well if you have not taken the time to teach him the steps to take to do a good job. Don't be a perfectionist; be a realist with your child.

5. Let go of your desire to control.

Give your child freedom to be and to grow. Remember the goal of discipline is *self*-control. If you are doing a good job of parenting, you are working your way out of a job by transferring control to your child little by little.

6. Practice focusing on the positives.

Look for the positives in your child and then express those positives to your child. The entire next project will teach you skills in this area.

Sometimes parents criticize, judge, or condemn their children when they need to be working on the above causes that are behind the criticism. As parents apply the above principles, they will be more positive and less sarcastic, critical, or condemning.

There *are* appropriate times to deal with negatives. You do need to be genuine and honest with your child. But a child needs to be confronted with the same kind of love you would confront your close friend—with sensitivity, and at the appropriate time.

III. Evaluation.

On the following scales circle the number that indicates where you generally are in each of these categories:

Do you state your needs to your child?

Always									Never
1	2	3	4	5	6	7	8	9	10

When you are upset about other problems do you tell your children how you are feeling?

Always									Never
1	2	3	4	5	6	7	8	9	10

When your children misbehave, do you take action?

Always									Never
1	2	3	4	5	6	7	8	9	10

Do you know the developmental tasks and skills your children are capable of at each of their age levels?

Yes									No
1	2	3	4	5	6	7	8	9	10

Do you spend time instructing and teaching your children how to do things before you correct them?

Always									Never
1	2	3	4	5	6	7	8	9	10

Do you control behaviors in your child that he should have control of himself at his age?

Yes   No
1   2   3   4   5   6   7   8   9   10

What do you see first in your child?

Positive   Negative
qualities   qualities
1   2   3   4   5   6   7   8   9   10

If you find that sometimes you give negative reflections to your children, which do you think usually causes those negative reflections?

☐ I learned negative patterns from my childhood.
☐ I sometimes get frustrated in other areas of my life and take it out on those around me.
☐ I use words to correct my children and do not take enough action.
☐ I need to learn more skills in how to discipline and handle my children.

What was the most important thing you learned in this project?

Let's look at the positive side of things! Make seven positive statements about yourself as a parent.

1.

2.

4.

5.

6.

7.

Recognize and Affirm Positive Traits in Your Child

I. Four ways to give positive reflections to children.

Reflecting positive qualities to your children is one of the strongest ways to build a positive self-image in your children.

There are four specific ways that parents can mirror or reflect the positives that they see in their children. They can . . .

1) Affirm positive character traits
2) Verbalize positive growth
3) Visualize success
4) Praise accomplishments, efforts, and work

STEP 1 Affirm positive character traits.

Affirming your child's positive character traits means to look for the positive character traits in your child's life and then tell him the positive traits that you see.

Children with positive characteristics might be:

cheerful	honest
compassionate	humorous
cooperative	kind
courageous	loyal
courteous	neat
creative	obedient
curious	organized
decisive	patient
efficient	peacemaker
enthusiastic	punctual
fair-minded	respectful
flexible	responsible
forgiving	self-disciplined
friendly	shares well
fun	sincere
generous	sympathetic
grateful	tender
hard worker	wise
helpful	understanding

You can affirm positive character traits by using the following formula:

> "You were . . ."
> (*name specific character trait*)
> " . . . when you . . ."
> (*describe the specific incident*).

Study the following examples. The specific character trait is printed in bold letters and the incident that affirmed the trait is italicized:

"You were **very responsible** when you *put your toys away before I even got home.*"

"You were **very cooperative** in school today when *the teacher put you in a group that you did not like.* You showed a **good attitude** and **cooperative spirit.**"

"I noticed that **being fair** was important to you when *you told the boys to play by the rules with Jimmy or you would not play.*"

"You were **very forgiving** when *Bob came to the door and asked you to forgive him; I know he really hurt you.* You were very **loving** to forgive him."

"You were **very patient** when *I was talking to Jane.* Thank you. I know it was a long time that you waited for me."

Affirm specific positive traits with proof (sharing an example). Do not affirm or praise general character like "You are a good girl," or "You are such an angel." When a child is praised with blanket statements like these, his self-esteem is lessened because he cannot live up to statements of general character all the time. The child thinks of the exceptions and knows he is not always that way.

Practice affirmations. In each of the examples below, write the exact words you would say to the child to affirm him, using the formula above.

1. Your three-year-old received a box of candy as a present from her grandma. She shares it with her friends in the neighborhood.

   You say,

2. It's August. Your child has complained of boredom throughout the past two weeks. Today, without prompting, he gets his library card and asks permission to walk to the library. (The library is nearby and he is capable of walking there alone.)

   You say,

3. Your two boys have been arguing over who gets the ten-speed bike this afternoon. You overhear the older boy say, "Okay, Tim, you can have it this time, but I get it tomorrow afternoon."

   You say,

4. You accidently meet your boss at a shopping center. You introduce him to your eight-year-old son. Your son shakes hands with him, looks him right in the eye, and says, "Hi." You have been trying to teach your son how to greet adults.

You say,

STEP 2 *Verbalize positive growth.*

As you watch your child grow, identify areas where he is growing. Then, point out those areas to him as you see him changing and growing in positive ways.

1. Verbalize areas of *physical growth* and development:
   "You can tie your shoes! How you are growing!"

2. Verbalize areas of *social growth:*
   "You are improving in your manners. I saw that you put your napkin in your lap without being reminded."

3. Verbalize areas of *intellectual growth:*
   "First semester you got a "C" in math and this semester you got a "B." You have improved; that's great!"

4. Verbalize areas of *character growth:*
   "You have been ready to go on time the last two times we went to church. That's great! You are improving on being punctual."

STEP 3 *Visualize success.*

Being a parent is like coaching—you teach your children skills, help them practice those skills, and then send them out to play the game, saying, "You can do it!"

Saying, "You can do it!" is visualizing success for your child. You believe he can do it. If you don't, he won't believe in himself. He can fail by not believing he is capable—and because initially you didn't believe in him.

The following statements are examples of visualizing success for your children:

To a fifth grader who got a bad grade on the last test in science, "You can do better next time. I know you can. You just need some extra study skills. I can teach you how to study for tests."

To a six-year-old, "I know you want to meet the new girl across the street. Just go over and knock on the door and ask if she wants to play. You may feel a little shy, but you can do it."

"Son, if you want to buy a bike, I know you can save and do it. Let's figure out how long you'll have to save your allowance. Maybe you could do some odd jobs to earn money."

When visualizing success for your child . . .

1) Be realistic about your child's capabilities. Don't push him into things that are too difficult for him. But do look at the potential that he has, but is not using.
2) Coach your child. Drawing upon your knowledge and experience, teach your child skills that he needs in order to succeed.
3) Be sensitive to when to push and when to wait for a readiness time. This can be done as you spend quality time with your child, know him well, and understand how he thinks and feels.
4) When your child sets goals that are really important to him, support him in that goal. It may seem like an unimportant goal to you—or even undesirable. But if your child wants to achieve that goal, believe in him. That's one of the greatest ways to nurture him!

STEP 4 *Praise accomplishments, efforts, and/or work.*

Step 1 discussed affirming specific positive character traits. You can affirm a child's character by expressing to the child the "facts" of what you see in him, with "proof" (the incident illustrating the good quality).

Affirming character traits (Step 1) is validating what is already there. Praising, however, does not involve character traits; it involves showing appreciation or enjoyment of a child's efforts, accomplishments, or work.

In giving praise, again it is important to be specific. For example:
   "You really worked hard on your piano piece for this week. It sounds beautiful! You got the rhythm down well."
   "I appreciate your hard work on the yard this morning."

"Your teacher told me today that you can read 56 words. I'm proud that you are learning how to read so many words."

II. Practicing Positive Reflections with Your Children

The following exercise will help you apply four ways of reflecting positives to *your* children. Do this exercise for each child over two years old. If you have additional children, use a separate piece of paper for your responses. You might find it easier to do only one page at a sitting, spending at least 15 minutes on each child.

A. Reflecting positives to (child's name):

_____ Age:_____

1. Look over the list of positive character traits on page 71. Then list at least four positive character traits for this child:

List two areas in which your child has worked hard, put forth an effort, or accomplished something positive. (Consider skills or activities the child has been involved in at home, at school, in church, etc.)

List two or more areas where your child has been growing—physically, socially, intellectually, or in his character.

List some areas (a) in which your child has goals at this time or (b) in which your child is struggling.

2. Using the above information, plan positive reflections that you can mirror to this child. Think of the exact words that you could say to the child and write those words below.

Statement 1:

Statement 2:

Statement 3:

Statement 4:

Statement 5:

B. Reflecting positives to (child's name):

_____ Age:_____

1. Look over the list of positive character traits on page 71. Then list at least four positive character traits for this child:

List two areas in which your child has worked hard, put forth an effort, or accomplished something positive. (Consider skills or activities the child has been involved in at home, at school, in church, etc.)

List two or more areas where your child has been growing—physically, socially, intellectually, or in his character.

List some areas (a) in which your child has goals at this time or (b) in which your child is struggling.

2. Using the above information, plan positive reflections that you can mirror to this child. Think of the exact words that you could say to the child and write those words below.

Statement 1:

Statement 2:

Statement 3:

Statement 4:

Statement 5:

The last step in this project is to tell your children the words that you wrote at the bottom of the preceding exercises. Plan to give one positive reflection to each child every day for seven days.

Record several positive reflections that you planned and told your children. Then write what you felt was the child's response.

Statement 1

To:

Words you used:

Child's response:

Statement 2

To:

Words you used:

Child's response:

Statement 3

To:

Words you used:

Child's response:

Note: Give lots of *extra* positive reflections to your child when he is really discouraged, when he fails, or when he is going through difficult times.

Project 20

Know Your Child and His Uniqueness_____

To build your child's self-esteem (the child's view of himself or herself), you must *know* your child—character, personality, likes and dislikes, thoughts and feelings. Only by knowing your child as a unique human being can you respond honestly and build him or her up in meaningful ways.

I. Study your child.

Select one of your children to study for this project. Consider the child whose temperament seems most different from yours or the child that you work hardest relating to. Write the child's name below. Then fill in the information requested.

Child's name: _____Age:_____

List the first three or four words that come to your mind in describing this child:
1.
2.
3.
4.

Two favorite toys are:
1.
2.

When the child chooses an activity or play, what does he or she do?
1.
2.
3.
4.

What are some things this child does well? Any special talents or abilities?

Complete the following statement

with the first things that come to your mind.
Doesn't like:
1.
2.
3.

What does this child want to be when he or she grows up?

Some scary things:

Which tendency does this child have? (Check one.)
☐ leader
☐ follower

Child's favorite foods:

Does the child have a hero? If so, who?

Positive character traits:

Negative character traits:

Think about how this child is on the "inside." What are some dreams, desires, and feelings that she or he has but may not share very much?

II. Interview your child.

Another way to understand more about your child's world is just to have the child tell you some things about what she or he thinks or feels.

Using the list of sentence starters on the next page, select a child (age three or over) to interview. Explain that you want him to finish the sentence with the first thing that comes into his mind. If he has two or three answers for any statements, write all answers down. When you are done, this interview can be used again for another child by using the second column. (Do not interview two children at the same time or the first child's responses will influence the second child.)

III. The real meaning of Proverbs 22:6.

Every child who is born into this world is a totally unique individual. There will never be another child like him. He has his own unique characteristics, abilities, and personality.

When God gives you a child, you do not know him. You need to study him—his habits, likes, dislikes, personality, temperament, etc. As your child grows, you have the delightful privilege of discovering a whole new person.

The Bible instructs parents in the importance of knowing their child. The Biblical teaching is in a little

	Child's Name:	Child's Name:
I like to . . .		
Mothers are . . .		
My favorite food is . . .		
My best friend is . . .		
I like my best friend because . . .		
I'm afraid when . . .		
My favorite place is . . .		
Daddies are . . .		
Today I feel . . .		
I get mad when . . .		
The best thing about my home is . . .		
If I were a parent, I would . . .		
I love to . . .		
My favorite toy is . . .		
My father . . .		
My mother . . .		
I don't like . . .		
I wish people wouldn't . . .		
When I grow up, I . . .		
When I'm alone, I . . .		
I don't like it when . . .		
It's hard for me to . . .		
I hate it when . . .		
I wish I could . . .		
I feel happiest when . . .		
I feel important when . . .		
I felt like crying when . . .		
If I were a teacher, I would . . .		
What I want most is . . .		
I feel proud when . . .		
Something that bothers me is . . .		
I'm good at . . .		
The most important person in the world is . . .		

verse tucked in Proverbs that is often misinterpreted—Proverbs 22:6. It says,

_____   _____

_____   _____

_____   _____

"Train up a child in the way he should go; and when he is old, he will not depart from it."

_____   _____

_____   _____

_____   _____

As the words that are circled are defined, write the Hebrew meanings in the spaces provided near the words:

The words *train up* mean to dedicate or give instruction to.

In means in keeping with, in accordance to, in cooperation with.

Way means a course of life, a mode of action, or characteristics or bents.

And *go* means by appointment, or according to.

When you put those Hebrew word meanings all together the verse could be read this way: "Train up or give instruction to a child in keeping with, in accordance to, in cooperation with, the characteristics or bents that he will meet by appointment or the

characteristics or bents that are predetermined."

The Amplified version of Proverbs 22:6 reads:
"Train up a child in the way he should go (and in keeping with his individual gift or bent), and when he is old he will not depart from it."

In order to train a child according to the way God made him with his bents for good and for evil, a parent must know what those characteristics are.

You discovered in the first section of this book that God gave a set of general instructions about raising children. There are certain needs that all children have for love and for discipline. But God did not give us a specific set of guidelines for each individual child.

God reveals specific guidelines to us as we study each child. Then we *can* know each child's tendencies and make plans for how to train the child up according to how God made him or her.

All children have bents toward good—good characteristics that they have inherently. Perhaps they are sensitive to others or have a good sense of humor, or find it easier to obey than some of their siblings.

All children also have bents toward evil—negative characteristics that they find difficult to control. They may tend to be dishonest or lazy or insensitive to others. These traits are negative and yet can be predominant in the child's life.

Before considering bents for good and for evil that a child can have, take some time and look at yourself. List some positive qualities that you have that seem to be

inherent. They are characteristics that have come naturally and that you have had most of your life.
1.

2.

3.

Now list some negative qualities or characteristics that you have had to deal with most of your life.
1.

2.

3.

IV. Create a plan to apply Proverbs 22:6

Apply this command to the child you have selected at the beginning of this project.

STEP 1

Review the information that you filled out about your selected child on page 75. Then from those ideas, begin to complete the first column of the "Know Your Child" chart on the following page.

Consider characteristics of the child and decide whether each characteristic is positive or negative. As you discover positive characteristics, write them in the first column in the top chart. As you discover negative characteristics, write them in the first column in the bottom chart.

KNOW YOUR CHILD

Positive bent, tendency, characteristic, talent, or ability.	Specific plan to encourage and develop each positive bent.
1.	
2.	
3.	
4.	

Negative bent, tendency, or characteristic.	Specific plan for discouraging growth of these negative tendencies.
1.	
2.	
3.	
4.	

Example of positive characteristic:

Sociable – enjoys being with friends.	– Allow her to have friends overnight often. – Be friendly to her friends and welcome them.

Example of negative characteristic:

Slow – takes too long to get dressed in morning.	– Wake her up earlier. – Allow more time for her to get ready. – Have her clothes set out the night before.

Your child may have some characteristics or natural bents which you did not write down at the beginning of this project. Consider the list of possible positive traits found on page 71, as well as the following list of possible negative tendencies. Add any predominant positive or negative characteristics that this child has on the "Know Your Child" chart.

Possible negative tendencies:

aggressive	manipulative
close-minded	mean
conceited	messy
critical	never on time
demanding	outspoken
dishonest	overly serious
domineering	perfectionistic
hates work	proud
headstrong	stingy
impatient	stubborn
indecisive	too competitive
inflexible	too talkative
insensitive to others	touchy
	unforgiving
irresponsible	ungrateful
lacks manners	unkind
lazy	unloving

Usually you will be listing character traits like the ones listed above or on page 71; however, your child might have a habit or a pattern of behavior that is either positive or negative (e.g., "chews his nails"). You may want to list these, too.

STEP 2

Look at the right-hand column on the "Know Your Child" chart. The column at the top says, "Specific plan to encourage and develop each positive bent." The column for the negative traits says, "Specific plan for discouraging growth of these negative tendencies."

Fill in this side of the chart and create a plan for as many character traits or bents that you can. Study the sample chart above for ideas of how to make plans.

STEP 3

Put your plan into effect. As you do, you will be training your child according to his own particular uniqueness.

Then three to four months later, return to this chart and evaluate what kind of changes have taken place in your child as a result of this plan.

STEP 4

At a later date, when you have put this plan into effect with one child, use a separate piece of paper and identify positive and negative characteristics with your other children and make plans to train them up according to their unique bents for good and for evil.

Give Your Child Focused Attention

"Many parents are with their children physically, but mentally their focus is elsewhere. Togetherness without genuine encounter is not togetherness at all."[1]

Everyone wants someone to "look" at him—totally, completely, without distractions. A child who receives short periods of focused attention feels loved and cherished during that time. It is true that children need bigger doses of our time and attention, but giving focused attention for a few minutes each day is crucial to a child's self-esteem. You can give your child a few minutes of focused attention no matter how busy you are!

Dorothy Briggs in her book *Your Child's Self-Esteem* discusses focused attention and calls it "genuine encounters," which she defines as " . . . attention with a

special intensity born of direct, personal involvement."[2] She continues to say that "the opposite of genuine encounter involves distancing. You do not focus attention intimately; you hold back. You see but from a distance, avoiding personal engagement."[3]

I. Who Cared?

When you were a child, who was one adult who really listened to you and seemed to care about you?

A. What indicated that this person cared about you?

B. How did you feel while you were with this person?

C. Did you share more of your life with this adult than with anyone else?

☐ Yes ☐ No   If yes, why?

When you were a child who were some adults that seemed more distant with you, not really there or caring?

How did you feel when you were with these adults?

	Genuine encounters with your child	Distant encounters with your child
Parent's Mind	Mind focused on the child Ready to receive what the child has to say Does not allow any distractions for this short period of time Listens without thinking what he is going to say while the child talks	Mind may be focused on a problem, thought, or concern—not child Distracted easily Difficult to keep mind tuned to the child
Parent's Words	Positive, loving words Soft, pleasant tone of voice At times might use firm tone of voice, but never harsh Seeks to communicate fully with child and understand child's concerns	May ask child to repeat what he says Indifference to child's sharing Not responsive to help child with his concern or share his excitement Sometimes monotone or irritated tone of voice
Parent's Nonverbal Communcation	Looks directly into child's eyes Gets on child's eye level Pleasant facial expressions Body posture toward child Loving gestures (hands on child's shoulder, hugs, etc.)	Eyes wander from child to other things Body posture away from child (back to child, reads magazine or newspaper, etc.) Facial expressions indifferent or unpleasant

II. Are your encounters with your children genuine or distant?

When your child comes to you and begins to communicate, how do you respond? Are you ready to really listen, or are you distant and remote? The chart on the preceding page describes the difference between the two types of encounters.

When your child comes to you and wants to talk for a short period of time, if you genuinely look at your child and focus on him, he feels loved, special, encouraged, and satisfied. However, if you are distant and remote from your child when he comes to you, the child feels frustrated, disappointed, ignored, and perhaps in the way.

If a child constantly, over a long period of time, receives distancing he will also feel rejected, cheated, anxious, and bitter. If a child is receiving a lot of encounters that indicate a remoteness and distance between him and his parent, he will have negative feelings about himself. He will not feel important. His self-esteem will be poor because he sees his importance based on how you, his parent, feel about him.

Which type of encounters are you having with your child on an overall basis? Read over the chart contrasting genuine encounters with distant encounters. Rate your encounters with each of your children. Are your encounters genuine or distant?

Child's name:_____

Distant encounters							Genuine encounters		
1	2	3	4	5	6	7	8	9	10

Child's name:_____

Distant encounters							Genuine encounters		
1	2	3	4	5	6	7	8	9	10

Child's name:_____

Distant encounters							Genuine encounters		
1	2	3	4	5	6	7	8	9	10

What would you like to do to improve your encounters with your children?

III. Practicing genuine encounters.

As you look over your rating of genuine encounters for each child, select one child who seems to receive fewer genuine encounters. Use the following evaluations to practice and improve the kinds of encounters that you have with that child.

Child selected: _____

Using the three forms provided, begin practicing genuineness in your encounters with the child you have selected. Use the first two forms to rate yourself. Then ask your spouse or a friend to observe and evaluate you for the last encounter. (If you are not aware of the times they are evaluating you, it will be a better evaluation.)

Evaluate short encounters of two to four minutes. Check the appropriate column as each characteristic is rated.

Encounter one (2-4 minutes)
Observed and rated by _____
Encounter between
(child) _____
and (parent) _____

	Poor	Satisfactory	Excellent
Looks directly into child's eyes	☐	☐	☐
Gets on child's eye level	☐	☐	☐
Pleasant facial expressions	☐	☐	☐
Body posture toward child	☐	☐	☐
Loving gestures, appropriate to child's age (hugs, touching, etc.)	☐	☐	☐
Positive loving words	☐	☐	☐
Pleasant tone of voice	☐	☐	☐
Seeking with words to communicate fully with child	☐	☐	☐
Seeks with words to understand child's concerns	☐	☐	☐
Mind focused on the child	☐	☐	☐
Ready to receive what the child has to say	☐	☐	☐
Does not allow distractions while talking	☐	☐	☐

Encounter two (2-4 minutes)	Poor	Satisfactory	Excellent
Observed and rated by _____			
Encounter between			
(child) _____			
and (parent) _____			
Looks directly into child's eyes	☐	☐	☐
Gets on child's eye level	☐	☐	☐
Pleasant facial expressions	☐	☐	☐
Body posture toward child	☐	☐	☐
Loving gestures, appropriate to child's age (hugs, touching, etc.)	☐	☐	☐
Positive loving words	☐	☐	☐
Pleasant tone of voice	☐	☐	☐
Seeking with words to communicate fully with child	☐	☐	☐
Seeks with words to understand child's concerns	☐	☐	☐
Mind focused on the child	☐	☐	☐
Ready to receive what the child has to say	☐	☐	☐
Does not allow distractions while talking	☐	☐	☐

Encounter three (2-4 minutes)	Poor	Satisfactory	Excellent
Observed and rated by _____			
Encounter between			
(child) _____			
and (parent) _____			
Looks directly into child's eyes	☐	☐	☐
Gets on child's eye level	☐	☐	☐
Pleasant facial expressions	☐	☐	☐
Body posture toward child	☐	☐	☐
Loving gestures, appropriate to child's age (hugs, touching, etc.)	☐	☐	☐
Positive loving words	☐	☐	☐
Pleasant tone of voice	☐	☐	☐
Seeking with words to communicate fully with child	☐	☐	☐
Seeks with words to understand child's concerns	☐	☐	☐
Mind focused on the child	☐	☐	☐
Ready to receive what the child has to say	☐	☐	☐
Does not allow distractions while talking	☐	☐	☐

In what ways have you improved in quality encounters with your children as a result of completing this project?

As you continue to grow in quality time with your child, practice genuine encounters . . .

. . . during the last few minutes in the morning before your children go to school.

. . . for the first few minutes when your children return home from school.

. . . anytime your child is upset and comes to you with a problem or hurt (physical or emotional).

. . . for the first few minutes of *any* encounter with your child.

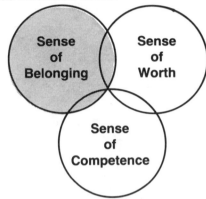

Develop Your Child's Sense of Belonging

If a child has a positive self-image, he will have a sense of belonging, competence, and worth as illustrated below:

Sense of Belonging / **Sense of Worth** / **Sense of Competence**

You cannot really separate one area from another. However, for the sake of gathering as many practical skills as possible, each of the next three projects will focus on one of these three dimensions of self-esteem.

I. How to develop a sense of belonging in your children.

Possessing a sense of belonging means having a sense of security and identity with others who love you.

Security includes feeling safe, cared for, unworried, and sheltered.

Identity includes feelings of kinship, likeness, sameness, and oneness.

In contrast, a child with a poor self-image feels insecure, which may include feeling unsafe, threatened, unsupported, alone, afraid, anxious, or fearful of new experiences.

A child with a poor self-image also feels a lack of identity, which includes feelings of differentness, discrepancies, inequality, or distance between himself and those who love him.

II. What can parents do to build a sense of belonging in their children?

The greatest influence on a child's sense of belonging comes from the child's relationship with his parents.

1. *Keep your priorities straight* so that you have time for your children.
2. *Spend quality time* when you can give your child focused attention.
3. *Cherish your child;* treat him special. Your child is a gift to you from God; do not take him for granted.
4. *Express love verbally* to your child. Some people never remember their mother or father saying, "I love you." Children need to be honestly loved and told, "I love you."
5. *Express love nonverbally* by giving your child hugs, kisses, pats on the back, etc.
6. *Meet your child's needs.* Put yourself in your child's place often to help you be aware of your child's concerns and needs. Then take action to meet any needs your child has—whether they are physical, emotional, intellectual, or spiritual needs.
7. *Model openness and honesty.* Your children will be more open and honest with you because

they will feel that you may be able to understand their feelings.
8. *Discipline your child.* The Bible teaches that one who really belongs in a family is loved so much that he is disciplined. Discipline is a sign of belonging (Hebrews 12:8).
9. *Share some of your feelings and struggles* with your child when appropriate. Let your child know that you have feelings similar to his. Share positive ways you have learned to deal with these feelings.
10. *Build relationships* in your life that give you a sense of belonging so that you experience it yourself and know the satisfaction it gives.

III. Develop your child's sense of belonging within the family.

Not only does a child need to feel safe and secure in his relationship with you, he also needs to feel secure in the family setting. There are several ways to accomplish this.

1. *Include all of your children in family communication.* Don't let more aggressive children overpower more passive or younger children. If you have one child who generally gives his opinion on any subject, say, "What do *you* think?" to each of your other children. Develop a pattern of getting responses from all of your children, not just the verbal or outspoken ones.
2. *Never allow one child to verbally tear down a sibling.* Consistently enforcing this rule at mealtime will increase positive communication between siblings at other times.

If one child calls another child

a name or speaks without respect, explain that the next time he attacks his brother or sister at mealtime, he will be asked to leave the table.

When you express how much you value each child by not allowing one child to tear down another, you establish that each child belongs there and will be protected and cared for. You will not allow one child to hurt another because you care for all of them.

3. *Give your children responsibilities at home.* Working in a home and caring for it gives a child a feeling that it is his and he belongs there. He needs that sense of teamwork: "We're all in this together," and "We all need to do our part to care for our home."

Sometimes parents are lax in giving chores to their children. One of the greatest results of establishing chores is that the child has a new sense of belonging because he shares in the responsibilities. He may not like the work, but psychologically he feels better because he feels that he belongs.

4. *Don't show favoritism.* Give children love and respect equally. Good parents can favor one child and be unaware of it. A parent usually does not do it purposefully. So evaluate carefully if you are favoring:
   • the youngest child;
   • a child with the same temperament as you have; or
   • a child who is the same sex as you.

5. *Every child should have some possessions of his own.* As an adult, you decide whether you want to share your possessions—your car, house, tools, etc. Children need that right. That doesn't mean that they can't share their toys. It just means that there are a few special toys that can be put away when company comes if they don't want to share them.

6. *Children need a place of their own.* Even if two or three children share a room together, there can be designated areas for each child. If quarrels are frequent about how rooms are kept or whose space is whose, mark off each child's area with masking tape.

Each child then has a space that he is responsible for, a "place" of his own which he can keep as neat as he desires (sometimes despite a messy sister or brother). He also can arrange his own furniture and possessions within that space. It is truly his space. Having one's own space, no matter how small it is, gives a child a sense that he belongs there.

IV. Developing your child's sense of belonging with others.

A. *Develop your child's sense of belonging with your friends.*
• Always introduce your children to your friends. No matter how young they are, your children are people and deserve courtesy and respect by being introduced.
• At appropriate times, encourage your children to share their interests, activities, and achievements with your friends who show an interest in your children.
• As you establish relationships between your children and your friends, you are giving your child other adults to relate to when they are teens and need to seek out others for advice.
• However, children do not need to monopolize adult conversations. Keep some prime time for you and your spouse alone and also some time for other adult relationships.

B. *Develop your child's sense of belonging with his friends.*
• Teach your child how to be a good friend. Encourage your child to have close as well as casual friendships as he gets into the middle elementary grades. Teach him how to handle both types of relationships and the value of having both.
• Keep your home open to your child's friends. A child has a sense of belonging when he can bring his friends home and they are welcome there. Provide limitations (of space, rooms, or rules) so that your needs are cared for, but within those limitations be loving and accepting of your child's friends.
• Encourage your child when he is going through hard times in friendships. Don't try to solve his problems for him, but give him encouragement and help him think of creative solutions to his problems.

C. *Develop your child's sense of belonging in the neighborhood.*
As our society is increasingly more mobile, it becomes more difficult to sense that you "belong" in a certain neighborhood. Neighborhoods can change many times in one's lifetime.

First, develop your own sense of belonging by getting acquainted and being friendly with your neighbors. Provide time in your conversations for your children to get acquainted, too.

Encourage your child to help your neighbors by doing jobs for them that will help them, such as baby-sitting, mowing lawns, running errands, dog walking, shoveling snow, leaf raking, car washing, etc.

Your child could even make up a flier and list the jobs he is willing to do with the amounts he will charge for each job, and then distribute the fliers to neighbors.

As your child works for people in your neighborhood, he will be able to say "Hi!" to more of them as he walks down his street and feel he really belongs in his neighborhood.

One neighborhood problem to consider is what to teach your child about the neighborhood "bully." Most neighborhoods have one.

(a) Teach your child to have compassion for all of his peers, even though he may not choose them for friends. Help him to realize some of the influences on children that cause them to be aggressive and angry with other people.

(b) Teach your child that it is wise to not antagonize aggressive individuals.

(c) Teach your child to choose his close friends carefully because friends influence us in many ways.

D. *Develop your child's sense of belonging with his relatives.*

Because our society is so mobile, it is more difficult to maintain close relationships with relatives. But these relationships give a child a sense of roots—where he has come from.

Many times children especially cherish their relationship with their grandparents. If your parents want to have more time with their grandchildren, encourage your child to spend weekends (if they live close) or a few weeks in the summer (if they live far away) with his grandparents.

If you are a single parent, be sure to give your child an opportunity to develop relationships with adults of the same sex as the parent with whom the child is not living. This type of relationship is important for your child's development. Consider which of your relatives would be the kind of models you would like your children to relate to. Then plan special times with those relatives.

E. *Develop your child's sense of belonging in your church.*

Children generally spend two to four hours a week with their church friends. In contrast, they may spend 25 to 30 hours a week in school.

They also spend many hours a week playing with their friends in the neighborhood.

Close friendships require time to get better acquainted, to share common activities. If children do not spend much time with friends from their church, we cannot expect close friendships to develop.

Suggest that your child invite a church friend to stay overnight during a weekend or to come home with him on Sunday afternoon. This extra playtime is crucial in developing stronger relationships with church friends.

V. Practical applications for your family

There are three tests included in this project. There are two copies of the first test. If you have more children, you will have to answer the questions on a separate piece of paper for each additional child. When you have completed the tests, compare the work sheets for each child. Evaluate whether you need to work with one child more intensively for a short period of time to build his sense of belonging.

TEST 1—YOU AND YOUR CHILD'S SENSE OF BELONGING.

Child: _____ Age:_____

1. What have you said or done during the last seven days to let this child know he or she is special?

2. How much time have you spent alone with this child during the last week? _____hours _____minutes

3. Name one particular physical need that this child had during the past week.

   What did you do to care for his or her physical need?

4. Name one emotional need that this child had during the past week.

85

What did you do to care for that emotional need?

5. How many times did you give five minutes (or more) of focused attention to this child during the past week? ☐ Many times a day. ☐ At least once a day. ☐ One or two times this week. ☐ Not at all. Describe one of those times.

6. Think of a time during the past week when you loved your child so much that you corrected this child to help him or her do the right thing. Describe that time and also state the action you took to correct him.

TEST 1—YOU AND YOUR CHILD'S SENSE OF BELONGING.

Child: _____ Age:_____

1. What have you said or done during the last seven days to let this child know he or she is special?

2. How much time have you spent alone with this child during the

last week? _____hours _____minutes

3. Name one particular physical need that this child had during the past week.

What did you do to care for his or her physical need?

4. Name one emotional need that this child had during the past week.

What did you do to care for that emotional need?

5. How many times did you give five minutes (or more) of focused attention to this child during the past week? ☐ Many times a day. ☐ At least once a day. ☐ One or two times this week. ☐ Not at all. Describe one of those times.

TEST 2—EVALUATING YOUR CHILDREN'S SENSE OF BELONGING IN THE FAMILY.

Write the names of each of your children in the space provided above the boxes on the right-hand side of this paper. Begin by writing the name of your oldest child.

If you have more than three children, line up a separate piece of paper with the edge of this book; then add columns on the extra papers for each additional child.

	Child #1	Child #2	Child #3
1. If you had a choice, which child would you select to take with you on errands?	☐	☐	☐
2. When you are on vacation, which child do you usually find special toys or mementos for first?	☐	☐	☐
3. With which child do you have the closest relationship?	☐	☐	☐
4. Which child's needs are you most aware of?	☐	☐	☐
5. Which child do you enjoy being with the most?	☐	☐	☐
6. Which child is the easiest to compliment?	☐	☐	☐
7. With which child do you spend the most time?	☐	☐	☐
8. Which child do you talk to the most?	☐	☐	☐
9. When you spend time playing with your children, which child do you enjoy playing with the most?	☐	☐	☐
10. Which child is the easiest to love?	☐	☐	☐

6. Think of a time during the past week when you loved your child so much that you corrected this child to help him or her do the right thing. Describe that time and also state the action you took to correct this child.

Evaluation of Test. Does one child have most of the checks? If so, look at life in the family from the child's point of view who had the *least* checks. Would he have a sense of belonging?

If you were the child with the least amount of checks, how would you feel?

If you have discovered through this evaluation that you tend to favor one child, consciously work toward eliminating this pattern from your parent-child relationships. Favoritism is common, even though parents usually don't mean to do it.

TEST 3—Evaluate how your children speak to each other.

Listen in on their conversations with each other. Write down any disrespectful remarks that they make to each other. At this time do not try to correct them, just unobtrusively listen and record at least five remarks or statements that were disrespectful. Keep this book handy during the next 24 hours and record the remarks exactly as they were said. After the

remark, write the name of the child who made the remark.

1.

2.

3.

4.

5.

If you discover a lot of disrespectful talk between siblings, you *can* stop it. You cannot supervise and stop all disrespectful remarks, but you can plan to stop them at the dinner table each evening.

You can put into effect a new rule by saying, "Every person at our dinner table will be treated with respect. There is to be no name calling, and no one can attack anyone else's character. If anyone violates this rule, he will be asked to leave the table and go to his

room during the remainder of the meal. That person will not be able to finish his meal and cannot have anything to eat until our next regular meal."

To enforce this rule, give a warning the first time a child calls another a name or attacks someone else's character. You can use the words above. The second time it happens take the prescribed action.

You can further develop your children's sense of belonging by not allowing your children to tear each other down in front of you. Do you feel that your family is at a place where they could benefit from the plan stated above? ☐ Yes ☐ No

Review how to develop a sense of belonging with others on pages 84 and 85. Then make a list below outlining three specific things you want to do to help your child have a sense of belonging with other people outside the immediate family. (Consider your friends, your children's friends, neighbors, relatives, and church friends.)

1.

2.

3.

Help Your Child Feel Capable

Can you recall a time when you worked hard on a specific job and had an "I did it!" feeling when you were done? It's a good feeling. There is satisfaction and fulfillment in using your potential to achieve a goal.

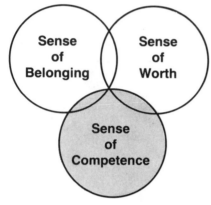

That's what this project is all about—how to build that "I did it!" feeling, a sense of competence, in your children.

Having a sense of competence means feeling adequate and capable; being able to achieve a desired goal. A child who has a sense of competence feels adequate, qualified, fit for the job, and that he has ample resources.

In contrast, a child who does not have a sense of competence feels inadequate and incapable; unable to achieve a desired goal.

As you recall, a parent greatly influences and affects a child's self-image. Parents are like mirrors. Children believe whatever kind of reflections their parents give them, positive or negative.

A parent who reflects "You can do it!" will have children who have confidence and believe that they have the capabilities to tackle life's challenges and frustrations.

Parents who give mostly negative reflections do not believe in their children, and those children do not believe in themselves.

This doesn't mean that we overlook our children's negative characteristics or do not confront our children at all. It means we give mostly positive reflections to our children; then at the appropriate time and with great love we confront our children tenderly. Galatians 6:1 in the *Amplified Bible* explains how to confront. It says, " . . . set him right and restore and reinstate him, without any sense of superiority and with all gentleness, keeping an attentive eye on yourself, lest you should be tempted also."

What can parents do to help their children feel capable?

1. Believe that your child is capable.

Your child has fantastic potential. In fact, children use much more of their potential ability than adults use. Don't underestimate your child's capabilities.

2. Give your child opportunities to explore and try out new skills and experiences.

If your child wants to go down the slide in the park, even though you think he is too little, let him (with careful and close supervision).

If your child wants to take tennis lessons, look for lessons geared to his age and take him.

If your child wants to walk to his new school alone, let him.

If your child wants to dial the telephone when you call Grandma, let him.

We are *not* saying you should let your child do whatever he wants without guidance or correction or regard for safety. We are saying you should let him learn "how" to do things and develop skills. Let

him learn *how* to dial Grandma's telephone number, but teach him not to play with the telephone whenever he wants.

Also, some new experiences will need parental supervision and/or limitations (like using power tools, knives, or other dangerous equipment or experiences). Be aware of the child's development. Know what he is capable of and what he is not capable of.

As children explore new interests, ask them to be prepared to remain committed to that class or activity until it is over. Also, if you have several children you may find that you are driving children to and from all kinds of lessons and activities. You may need to limit each child to one outside activity at a time.

What have you done to encourage your children to explore new skills and interests? List each of your children and some activities and interests that they have explored during the past six months.

Child 1:_____
   1.

   2.

Child 2:_____
   1.

   2.

Child 3:_____
   1.

   2.

Name the last time you

remember one of your children asking to pursue a new interest or skill.

How did you respond?

3. Verbally express encouragement to your children while they are exploring and trying out new skills and experiences.

Use encouraging words that say:

You can do it!
Very good.
That's great!
One more try and you'll make it.
Fantastic!
I knew you could do it.
That's the best you've ever done.
Much better!
You did it!
You worked hard. I'm proud of you.
Try it! You can do it.

In Project 18, page 66, you kept a record of words you said to one child for a 24-hour period of time. Read over your statements and note any short phrases or words of encouragement that you used on that day with that child.

4. Affirm specific abilities, skills, and talents which you see in your child.

Study your children and identify specific abilities, talents, and skills that they possess. Besides giving general words of encouragement, also give specific affirmations of skills and abilities.

For example:

"I've noticed that you can tie your shoes now. You do a good job of tying shoes."

"You are a good kicker for your soccer team."

"You do an excellent job of vacuuming."

Write down the name of one of your children (over three years old, if possible).
Child: _____

Brainstorm specific abilities, skills, or talents this child has and list at least three below:

1.

2.

3.

Write two statements that you could use with this child to affirm the above abilities.
Statement 1:

Statement 2:

Think of a time when someone affirmed a specific skill or ability you have.

a) What was the specific skill or ability that was affirmed?

b) How did you feel at that time?

5. Allow your child to make some decisions of his own and value those decisions.

Whether your child is two, five, ten, or in his teens, it is important that he has your respect to make some decisions. If children are not allowed to make decisions of their own, their growth is stifled.

When children make good decisions, they feel a sense of competence. When children make poor decisions and have to live with those decisions, they learn by the consequences how to make better decisions the next time.

If you have a child who has a strong will, that child *especially* needs to make decisions appropriate for his age level. Making some decisions helps him feel more in control of his life, and he needs that. Give him decisions that do not involve right or wrong, but instead involve preferences. For example:

- color and style of clothing;
- choices of food when you are out to eat;
- how he will spend part or all of his allowance;
- activities that he desires to participate in;
- selection of toys;
- arrangement of furniture and possessions in his room.

When children have the freedom to make certain decisions, sometimes it is hard to allow them to make a decision that is a poor one. It may be difficult to watch your five-year-old put 25¢ in a gum-ball machine for the chance that he might also get a special toy that is displayed. Your child might even put another 25¢ in, hoping to get the toy the second time, and end up with only one gum ball each time.

When your child returns to share his disappointment with you and says, "That's not worth it!" he is learning some things that will be valuable all of his life. If the child has learned something about money and gum-ball machines, he has not failed, but learned. It is important to respect him and let him live with his choices. Don't rescue him and give him more money. He also doesn't need a lecture at this time; just someone who will reflect his disappointed feelings and care.

Help your child develop his decision-making ability in more important matters by teaching him how to make good decisions. Guide him to:

(1) Brainstorm all the alternatives he has in a situation.
(2) List the pros and cons of each of the alternatives in the decision.
(3) Select one alternative and do it.
(4) After the decision, evaluate.

Evaluate two of your children and how much influence they are allowed in making decisions in their lives. Circle the number in each of the categories that indicates who makes the decisions in that category.

A. Oldest Child: _____

Selection of child's clothing:

Parent decides									Child decides
1	2	3	4	5	6	7	8	9	10

Selection of child's food when you are out to eat:

Parent decides									Child decides
1	2	3	4	5	6	7	8	9	10

Style of haircut:

Parent decides									Child decides
1	2	3	4	5	6	7	8	9	10

Outside activities that child participates in:

Parent decides									Child decides
1	2	3	4	5	6	7	8	9	10

How child spends his own money:

Parent decides									Child decides
1	2	3	4	5	6	7	8	9	10

Selection of gifts parent buys for child:

What parent wants to get									What child asks for
1	2	3	4	5	6	7	8	9	10

Select another child and circle responses below:

B. Child: _____
Selection of child's clothing:

Parent decides									Child decides
1	2	3	4	5	6	7	8	9	10

Selection of child's food when you are out to eat:

Parent decides									Child decides
1	2	3	4	5	6	7	8	9	10

Style of haircut:

Parent decides									Child decides
1	2	3	4	5	6	7	8	9	10

Outside activities that child participates in:

Parent decides									Child decides
1	2	3	4	5	6	7	8	9	10

How child spends his own money:

Parent decides									Child decides
1	2	3	4	5	6	7	8	9	10

Selection of gifts parent buys for child:

What parent wants to get									What child asks for
1	2	3	4	5	6	7	8	9	10

If you desire to use this scale with additional children, use a separate piece of paper and record each category and the number that you would circle.

Are there any changes that you would like to make in the amount or types of decisions you want your children to make?

6. Encourage your child to be independent.

Encourage independence by giving your child all the freedom that he can handle responsibly.

Do not overprotect your child, trying to shield him from fears you may have for him. It is important for parents to protect and care for their children, but if parents overprotect, the children become weak and unable to cope with life.

Parents should not overdo their control of children. Some adults are extremely strict and do not give the child the *opportunity* to develop inner controls. The child is not able to handle freedom because the parent hasn't given the freedom and taught the child how to handle it.

A child's normal pattern of growth is to increase in self-control as he grows older and be given more and more freedom as he matures. The projects in Section II of this book cover how to discipline a child and lead him towards inner controls and an ability to handle freedom. Project 15 discussed how to help children handle freedom and responsibility. Review the principles in the accompanying chart.

Don't be afraid to give your children all the freedom they want because, if you use the plan outlined in the chart, they will also be responsible. This plan gives hope and deals positively with children when they are not able to handle a specific freedom. There is no name-calling or words like, "I can't trust you"; instead, there are words like, "We'll try again later."

As you apply the six principles in this project, you will help your child feel that he is capable and competent. But there will be times that you will need to deal with your child's feelings of failure. Protect your child's self-esteem when he feels that he has failed.

1) Help him identify how he has grown from the experience and what he *has* learned.

2) Remind him of his successes and the capabilities that he does have.
3) If appropriate, redirect his attention and focus to help him get his mind off of feeling like a failure.
4) Don't cast blame when your child is just immature and inexperienced.
5) Don't be a perfectionist and demand perfection for success. That's discouraging!

Review the six principles in this project. What goals would you like to set to help your children develop a sense of competence?

1.

2.

3.

4.

5.

6.

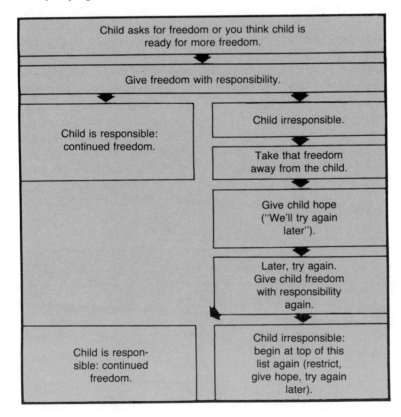

Child asks for freedom or you think child is ready for more freedom.

Give freedom with responsibility.

Child is responsible: continued freedom.

Child irresponsible.

Take that freedom away from the child.

Give child hope ("We'll try again later").

Later, try again. Give child freedom with responsibility again.

Child is responsible: continued freedom.

Child irresponsible: begin at top of this list again (restrict, give hope, try again later).

Discipline and How It Affects Your Child's Self-Worth

I. What is self-worth?

The third dimension of self-esteem is a sense of worthiness.

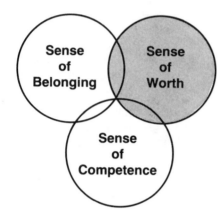

Dr. Maurice Wagner has defined *worthiness* in the following way: "Worthiness is a feeling of 'I am good' or 'I count' or 'I am right.' We feel worthy when we do as we should. . . . Worthiness is related to a sense of not only being right, but doing right. Self-control is important to worthiness."[1]

II. Who is responsible for a child "doing right"?

His parents! And who is responsible for developing a sense of self-control in a child? His parents!

The Scriptures we studied earlier verified that it is a parent's responsibility to correct his child:

"Discipline your son in his early years while there is hope. If you don't you will ruin his life" (Prov. 19:18, TLB).

"He who spares his rod hates his son, But he who loves him disciplines him diligently" (Prov. 13:24, NASB).

Children need parents to discipline them and thus build their self-discipline. The children will have a feeling of self-respect which comes with doing the right thing.

Dr. Wagner says, "Parental discipline is a necessity, brought upon the child by the nature of his own growth and the environmental situation in which he lives. . . . When the parents feel they must punish him for disobedience, the child's first inclination is to feel rejected, separated, and cut off from them. . . . As the parents consistently enforce their regulations, the child begins to learn to surrender his desired object to them and yield to their commands. When he does so, he is restored to their good graces and his separation anxiety is healed. He is again at peace with them. This is the essence of child training and emotional development.

"In the parents' loving forgiveness is restoration. Belongingness that was threatened is reaffirmed when correction is appropriate and fair. As belongingness is again and again restored and verified in parental discipline, a new sense of being somebody emerges which is called worthiness."[2]

Therefore, if you love your children greatly, you will also discipline them. That is the greatest kind of love—to know your child's nature and immaturity level, and then correct him when he needs it. Love that will go so far that it includes correction, builds the child's sense of worth. It is the kind of love that builds a child's self-esteem.

Discipline is proof of love. Without discipline a child cannot feel that he belongs and he cannot feel worthy.

III. Three stages of discipline

When you assume the job of parenthood, you need to recognize that you have the job of correcting the sinful nature of your children. As you do this, a sense of worth develops in your child.

Dr. Maurice Wagner suggests that there are three stages in this process: "standing against," "working with," and "withdrawing from" the child.

Put in chart form his suggestion might look like this:

The Three Stages of Discipline		
Stage 1	Preschooler, up to age three or four	"Stand against" child
Stage 2	Children, ages 4-13	"Work with" child
Stage 3	Teenagers, ages 13-18	"Withdraw from" child

Stage 1 of Discipline

Stage 1 of discipline is "standing against" or confronting children up to age three or four.

When preschoolers openly defy their parents' authority, the parent needs to firmly "stand against" the child's will. Children, ages two and three, will usually begin to strongly test their will against their parents.

At this time parents need to firmly take action to win these battles between the child's will and the parent's. Every battle won at age two or three in a child will help you avoid hundreds of battles in the future!

Preschoolers are not capable of understanding words and concepts enough to understand why their parents set limits. They have a limited understanding of the consequences of their misbehavior, future events related to their misbehavior, and a limited appreciation of other people's feelings and needs. Their experience, as well as their understanding, is limited. Therefore, reasoning with or trying to get a child to understand why he can't do things is an ineffective general pattern during Stage 1.

Stage 2 of Discipline

Stage 2 is "working with" children ages 4 through 13 years to help the child comply with the parent's will.

"Working with" involves knowing your child and his uniqueness and trying methods that will work to help your child obey. The parent still causes the child to obey, but he verbally helps the child to understand reasons why he should obey. The child may not always understand the reasons, but the parent will state the reason.

During this stage of "working with" children, the parent takes actions that will help the child cooperate. When the parent needs to overrule the child's will, the child knows deep inside that the parent loves him and that the rule is reasonable. (The child will also know if a rule is not reasonable and be offended.) You must love and cherish your child in order to be able to "work with" him.

Stage 2 includes much instruction and training—levels 1 and 2 of discipline. A parent needs to give explanations and reasons, and then set limits and enforce them.

Using logical consequences during this stage is very effective. In logical consequences the child makes a choice—that gives him room to grow in his understanding of the results of his choices. The parent maintains the authority when wrong choices are made and the negative consequences are carried out. In logical consequences the child sees a relationship between his behavior and the consequence, which helps him become wiser and accept more responsibility. There is much "working with" in the use of logical consequences.

Stage 3 of Discipline

Stage 3 of discipline involves "withdrawing from" the child during the teenage years of 13-18.

As the teenage years progress, the goal is to help the teenager become a fully functioning adult. Independence is the major developmental task of a teenager. Parents cooperate and work toward this developmental task by withdrawing during these years. This does not mean parents withdraw their love, attention, and support from teenagers. Parents of teenagers should withdraw more and more of their decision-controlling powers.

By the time a young person is 18-20 years old, he should be able to function as an adult in the home. If the child has matured as he should, there may be a few restrictions, but those restrictions have more to do with the parent's needs.

Parents set standards and morals that are important to them, no matter who is living in their home in order to be comfortable and continue to keep their home a "retreat" from the rest of the world. So, a young adult of 18 may need to comply with some standards because it is his *parents'* home—not his. If he refuses to honor his parents' home in this way, he should leave.

As you focus on the task of each stage, you will find child rearing easier. However, sometimes parents mix up the functions of each stage. Parents may "work with" preschoolers instead of "standing against" their defiant will. Or parents "stand against" teens and set restrictions that are too harsh and rigid and do not respect the child's person or age. At other times, parents can "withdraw from" children and not give them guidance when they desperately need it at their young age. All of these patterns are wrong.

If you have passed a certain stage with your child and have not completed the task for that stage, you cannot go back. You must do your best to restore the relationship now and resolve any grudges or hostilities that may remain from those previous stages. It involves doing everything possible to develop the highest quality of love in the relationship so that there may be freedom and motivation in the child to want to cooperate in the stage he is in now.

IV. Analyze these three stages of discipline and where your children fall in each of them.

(a) Review what you have learned so far by describing the parent's task at each stage in the chart below.

(b) In the second column write the names of each of your children

across from the appropriate stage.

(c) In the third column, note what you are doing to cooperate with this stage of discipline.

V. Discipline must be done with respect.

As a parent, you need to discipline your child to develop his self-esteem, but you must discipline in love and with respect.

Test yourself and see if you respect your children while disciplining them. Check your responses to each question that follows.

	Parent's task during this stage	Your children's names	What you are doing to cooperate with this stage
Stage 1 Preschooler, up to age three or four.			
Stage 2 Children, ages 4-13.			
Stage 3 Teenagers, ages 13-18.			

DO YOU RESPECT YOUR CHILD AS YOU DISCIPLINE HIM?

	Always	Usually	Sometimes	Rarely	Never
1. Do you embarrass your child in front of others in order to get him to behave?	☐	☐	☐	☐	☐
2. When you instruct and teach your child, do you act like he should already know things he hasn't been taught yet?	☐	☐	☐	☐	☐
3. Do you use your child as a poor example to others?	☐	☐	☐	☐	☐
4. Do you discuss your child's problems with other people?	☐	☐	☐	☐	☐
5. Do you yell or scream at your children?	☐	☐	☐	☐	☐
6. Do you use sarcasm when you correct your child?	☐	☐	☐	☐	☐
7. Do you threaten your child, but fail to follow through with action in discipline?	☐	☐	☐	☐	☐
8. Do you jump to conclusions too quickly?	☐	☐	☐	☐	☐
9. Do you lose your temper with your children?	☐	☐	☐	☐	☐
10. Are your rules for your benefit only?	☐	☐	☐	☐	☐
11. Do you call your children names?	☐	☐	☐	☐	☐
12. Do you overreact when problems arise?	☐	☐	☐	☐	☐
13. Do you spank your child when your anger is not under control?	☐	☐	☐	☐	☐
14. Do you spank your child in front of his peers?	☐	☐	☐	☐	☐
15. Have you ever spanked a teenager?	☐	☐	☐	☐	☐
16. Do you nag or belittle your child to get him to behave?	☐	☐	☐	☐	☐
17. Are you impatient with your child?	☐	☐	☐	☐	☐
18. Do you ignore your child and let him do whatever he wants rather than correct him?	☐	☐	☐	☐	☐
19. Do you use a harsh voice while correcting your child?	☐	☐	☐	☐	☐

Circle the numbers of the responses above that are in the "Always" and "Usually" columns.
Decide if you desire to make changes in your words or actions in any of these circled areas.
(You may also want to consider the "Sometimes" column.)

Always Believe in Your Child____

When you were a child, who was the person who believed in you, had confidence in you, and encouraged you the most?

Think of a specific time when this person encouraged you. Describe what that person did to show you that he or she believed in you.

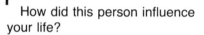

How did this person influence your life?

When someone loves and believes in us, we can believe in ourselves, despite circumstances that seem to tell us differently. We can develop our greatest potential because someone else believed that potential was there when we didn't believe in ourselves.

I. Four characteristics of real love.

The Bible tells us that there are four important characteristics of real love in I Corinthians 13:7:

"If you love someone you will be loyal to him no matter what the cost. You will always believe in him, always expect the best of him, and always stand your ground in defending him" (TLB).

The same verse in the King James Version says,

"[Love] . . . beareth all things, believeth all things, hopeth all things, endureth all things."

Loving your child involves all four of the following concepts:

BE LOYAL TO YOUR CHILD NO MATTER WHAT THE COST.

ALWAYS BELIEVE IN YOUR CHILD.

ALWAYS EXPECT THE BEST OF YOUR CHILD.

ALWAYS PERSEVERE NO MATTER HOW MUCH YOUR LOVE IS TESTED.

When you practice all four of these characteristics of love, that is the basis for developing a positive self-concept in your child.

A. *Always endure patiently with your child and be loyal to him.*

The first part of I Corinthians 13:7 says that "[love] beareth all things." *Bear* means to be patient and loyal when problems come.

As children go from babyhood to their teens, there are many times when we as parents need to patiently endure and be loyal to our children. At each age children go through various stages of development, some of which can be difficult. As we bear with our children, it is important to be loyal to them no matter what the cost.

For example, imagine that your boss or your pastor is visiting your home. Your child says something that is embarrassing to you. If you are loyal to your child you will not try to make yourself look better by tearing down your child. You will protect *your child's* reputation. You can (1) lovingly instruct the child, (2) correct him in private, or (3) ignore the problem and deal with it later, whichever approach is appropriate for the situation.

Knowing principles of discipline, methods to use, and a child's maturity level makes it easier to endure his behavior patiently because you know his need is for loving correction, and you know how to deal with it.

B. *Always believe in your child and give him credit.*

Underlying all our attitudes and behaviors in building self-esteem is believing the best of our children.

Believing means that you have confidence in your child. You believe he will do the right thing within his maturity level. You trust him. You give him credit.

Believe that your child can overcome weaknesses. If you do, he will have the strength to believe in himself. Let him know you have faith in him and you believe that his intentions are positive.

It is extremely discouraging not to be trusted. If you treat your child with mistrust and lack of confidence all the time, you will find your child so discouraged that he will become as bad as you think he is. Why not? Being condemned is discouraging, degrading, and deadening to anyone's spirit.

Believing and trusting in a child does not mean that you need to be naive about his weaknesses. Be realistic about your child's maturity level and inherent weaknesses. Don't naively put him in situations which he cannot handle.

The following statements reflect belief in a child:

"You will make it!"

"It won't be easy, but we can work through this."

"I know you are struggling with that problem, but you *can* overcome it."

In contrast, the following statements reflect distrust and lack of belief in a child:

"I'll never trust you again."

"When will you *ever* stop that behavior?"

"You'll never change."

C. *Always expect the best of your child.*

"Hopeth all things" (I Corinthians 13:7) means to anticipate with confidence. When you believe in someone, you expect the best from him. There is anticipation.

As your child encounters everyday situations, you expect that he will do his best. He may not always do his best, but you will expect him to—always! Instead of doubting his intentions, real love will have hope.

D. *Always endure with your child even in severe testing times.*

The last part of I Corinthians 13:7 says that love "endureth all things."

This phrase has a similar meaning to "bearing" all things. However, it is a stronger term. It means to *continue* to bear patiently, to *remain* firm under trials and testing.

A two-year-old child can be extremely frustrating as he continues to exercise his strong will. We sometimes stand amazed that such strength of will could be in such a little one! With other

children, severe testing of the relationship may happen during the elementary or teenage years.

It doesn't matter how old our child is, how terrible his behavior, or how difficult the problems are, our Heavenly Father instructs us to continue to love him and remain firm in our commitment to him under all trials and testing.

II. Practical applications: Affirming your love for your children.

What has been your greatest frustration and the most difficult thing to endure in your parenting so far?

What is another frustrating problem or experience you have had in your parenting?

The kind of love that bears all things, believes all things, hopes all things, and endures all things is a supernatural kind of love. It comes from God.

There will be times in your parenting when you feel that you do not have the resources to continue

MY COMMITMENT TO LOVE AND BELIEVE IN MY CHILDREN

Date_____

	Name of Each Child			
1. I will be loyal to this child no matter what the cost.	☐	☐	☐	☐
2. I will protect this child's reputation over my own reputation.	☐	☐	☐	☐
3. I will stay with this child no matter how frustrating his behavior gets.	☐	☐	☐	☐
4. I will continue to search for positive ways to deal with this child's frustrating behavior.	☐	☐	☐	☐
5. I will commit myself to always expect the best of this child.	☐	☐	☐	☐
6. I will bear patiently any trial or burden this child brings to me.	☐	☐	☐	☐
7. I will persevere with this child even if these trials increase and last a long time.	☐	☐	☐	☐
8. When I see weaknesses in this child, I will set appropriate limits to help him deal with those weaknesses and then trust him.	☐	☐	☐	☐

let alone continue with patience! Ask your Heavenly Father for His love and He will give you love—even for those difficult times when you are too frustrated to "endure" to the end! It is through His Spirit that you can best love your children.

Reaffirm your commitment to each of your children by checking the statements above prayerfully. If you cannot respond positively to some of the statements, leave your response blank and ask the Lord to help you with that area and bring you to a positive commitment.

Write a prayer to God thanking Him for the people in your life (during childhood *and* adulthood) who have believed in you and encouraged you by their love. Then ask God to help you be that kind of person in others' lives—especially in your children's lives.

PART FOUR

THE MOST IMPORTANT THING YOU CAN DO FOR YOUR CHILD

Keeping Things in Perspective

I. The marital life cycle.

Although there are many changes in marriage today with more divorces and more single parent homes, if a couple does stay married, they will spend considerable time in their marriage without children.

Studies have been conducted to explore the number of years a married couple spend together with and without children. Due to increased life expectancy and to changed fertility patterns in recent years, ". . . husbands and wives have many more years alone together without children. Increased life expectancy means more years together after retirement from paid work."[1]

How *much* time alone will couples spend in their marriage without children? ". . . couples marrying now are likely to spend nearly twenty-two years, almost half of their married life, alone together with no children in the house—mostly after the children are grown."[2]

If you remain married to your spouse, the amount of time with and without children could look like this:

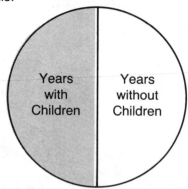

Therefore, approximately 50% of a couple's marriage is spent before children are born and after they leave home.

People who stay married have a greater amount of time alone, so it is crucial that they keep their relationship alive and growing when children come. *The most important family relationship is not the parent-child relationship, but the husband-wife relationship.*

The husband-wife relationship continues in intensity and intimacy, while the parent-child relationship will decrease in intensity and intimacy as children grow into adolescence and young adulthood, if the relationships develop as they should.

Children mature into young adults and become independent from their parents. When children marry, the Bible is clear about the relationship between grown married children and their parents:

"Therefore shall a man leave his father and his mother, and shall cleave unto his wife . . ." (Gen. 2:24).

"For this cause shall a man leave his father and mother and cleave to his wife . . ." (Mark 10:7).

Notice the words *leave* and *cleave. To cleave* means to cling, be joined together. Grown, married children are to cling closely to their spouse when they get married. They are also instructed to leave their parents. *To leave* means to forsake, or leave behind. It doesn't mean that there can't be a loving relationship. But it does mean that the spouse is the one that should be clung to for emotional, physical, and psychological support.

If parents neglect their marriage relationship, the results can be disastrous, and often show up when the last child leaves home.

"Mothers whose lives are

centered on their children might be expected to have considerable difficulty adjusting to married life without children. They may feel that their lives have no real purpose after they have raised their children . . . . Similarly, married couples may feel that they have little in common with each other once the bond created by children is gone."[3]

Parents sometimes wake up after their parenting years are over and the last child leaves home, look at their spouse and say, "Who are YOU??"

II. Seek to have a growing marriage.

Some preventative medicine is needed to keep your marriage and children in perspective *throughout* your married life. Be the best parent you can be, but do not neglect your relationship with your spouse. Seek to have a growing marriage. Realize that your relationship with your spouse should be one of your highest values and receive prime time in your life.

If you work toward a growing marriage and increasing intimacy, there will be many benefits for you:

- more fulfillment during the child-rearing years;
- personal enrichment through accepting your spouse's differences in temperament, personality, and natural characteristics;
- enjoyment of your spouse as an intimate friend;
- personal growth;
- an increasing sense of oneness through resolving conflicts and differences in the marriage;
- anticipation of time in the marriage without children.

You can help make your

marriage a growing marriage by:
1. respecting your mate;
2. increasing positive communication in your marriage;
3. spending quality fun time together without the children.

As we look at each of these last three areas, you will also evaluate and make personal plans for growth in these areas.

A. *Respect your mate.*

As stated earlier in parent-child relationships, respect is necessary in any relationship. *Respect* means to consider worthy of high regard or to esteem. Respect involves honoring each other, preferring, admiring, and loving each other.

Test yourself. How much do you respect your spouse? Read each question in the chart below, and check your response.

Circle the number of any responses that you would like to think about and consider changing.

How many questions did you circle? ___

Evaluate each of those circled questions. Select one to work on

DO YOU RESPECT YOUR SPOUSE?

	Always	Usually	Sometimes	Rarely	Never
1. Do you accept the differences in temperament and personality that your spouse possesses?	☐	☐	☐	☐	☐
2. Do you share with your spouse unique positive qualities that he/she possesses?	☐	☐	☐	☐	☐
3. Do you really listen when your spouse talks to you?	☐	☐	☐	☐	☐
4. Does your spouse feel free to express an opinion that is contrary to yours?	☐	☐	☐	☐	☐
5. When your spouse is angry, do you listen and try to understand the cause of the anger?	☐	☐	☐	☐	☐
6. Are you as careful in fulfilling your spouse's needs as you are in getting your own needs met?	☐	☐	☐	☐	☐
7. Do you encourage your spouse when he/she is discouraged?	☐	☐	☐	☐	☐
8. Do you try to control your spouse and get him/her to do what you feel is best?	☐	☐	☐	☐	☐
9. Are you supportive to your spouse when he/she is hurting emotionally?	☐	☐	☐	☐	☐
10. Are you as polite to your spouse as you are with other adults?	☐	☐	☐	☐	☐
11. Do you respect the decisions your spouse makes and support them?	☐	☐	☐	☐	☐
12. Do you make almost all of the decisions in your marriage?	☐	☐	☐	☐	☐
13. When you disagree with your spouse, do you try to make it look like your opinion is better than your spouse's?	☐	☐	☐	☐	☐
14. When someone asks your spouse a question, do you answer for him/her?	☐	☐	☐	☐	☐
15. Do you know your spouse's major concerns?	☐	☐	☐	☐	☐
16. Do you take the time and effort to help your spouse with his/her concerns in life?	☐	☐	☐	☐	☐
17. Do you encourage your spouse to engage in some activities of his/her own?	☐	☐	☐	☐	☐
18. Do you ask your spouse to forgive you when you are wrong?	☐	☐	☐	☐	☐
19. Do you encourage your spouse to be all he/she can be and develop to his/her fullest potential?	☐	☐	☐	☐	☐

during the next seven days. Write it here:

What are some specific things you could do to improve in this area during the next seven days?

As you look over any other circled statements, do you see other areas of change that you would like to make in the future? If so, write those changes here:

B. *Increase communication in your marriage.*

1. Begin by being positive. Don't continually nag, criticize, or reflect mostly negatives to your spouse or you will destroy your relationship.

So speak positively. Affirm your spouse's positive character traits by telling your mate the positives you see in his interactions with others, in his work and accomplishments, and in his efforts.

Test yourself. How positive are you with your spouse?

Read over your responses to the test on how positive you are. Select one category that you want to work on during the next seven days:

☐ Compliment your spouse;
☐ Share positive character traits that you see in your spouse;
☐ Encourage your spouse in his interests and hobbies;
☐ Say, "I love you";
☐ When your spouse is discouraged, try to encourage him/her;
☐ Thank your spouse for how he/she cares for family responsibilities.

List some habits, characteristics, or behaviors that your spouse has that you don't like.

When was the last time you . . .	Within the last 24 hrs.	Within the last seven days	Longer than seven days
. . . complimented your spouse?	☐	☐	☐
. . . shared a positive character trait that you saw in your spouse?	☐	☐	☐
. . . said, "I love you"?	☐	☐	☐
. . . encouraged your spouse in an interest or hobby of his/hers?	☐	☐	☐
. . . recognized that your spouse was discouraged and tried to encourage him/her?	☐	☐	☐
. . . thanked your mate for the family responsibilities that he/she does take?	☐	☐	☐

Do you constantly talk about, nag, or criticize any of the above?
☐ Yes   ☐ No

If so, how do you think that affects your marriage relationship?

WHAT KIND OF ENCOUNTERS DO YOU HAVE WITH YOUR SPOUSE?		
	Genuine encounters with your spouse	**Distant encounters with your spouse**
Your Mind	Mind focused on spouse Ready to receive what spouse has to say Does not allow any distractions for this short period of time Listen without thinking what you are going to say while your spouse talks	Mind may be focused on other problems, thoughts, or concerns—not on spouse Distracted easily Difficult to keep mind tuned to spouse
Your Words	Positive, loving words even in conflicts Seeks to communicate fully with spouse and understand spouse's concerns Pleasant tone of voice	May ask spouse to repeat what he/she says Indifference to spouse's sharing Not responsive to help spouse with his/her concerns and share in his/her excitement Sometimes monotone or irritated voice
Your Nonverbal Communication	Look directly into spouse's eyes Pleasant facial expressions Body posture toward spouse Loving gestures (holding hands, hugs, etc.) Sits near spouse	Eyes wander from spouse to other things Body posture away from spouse (back to spouse, reads newspaper or magazine, etc.) Facial expressions indifferent or unpleasant Sits far away from spouse

2. Seek genuine encounters with your spouse. You can increase communication in your marriage by working towards more genuine encounters with your spouse. Refresh the difference between genuine and distant encounters in your mind as you read over the above chart which has been adapted from Project 21 to relate to encounters with your spouse.

What kind of encounters have you had during the last 24 hours with your spouse?

Distant   Genuine
encounters   encounters
1 2 3 4 5 6 7 8 9 10

Begin practicing genuine encounters with your spouse during the first few minutes that you come together and the last few minutes before you leave each other. Check the areas below that you especially want to practice and improve in:

☐ Focus your mind on your spouse.
☐ Be ready to receive what your spouse has to say.
☐ Don't allow any distractions.
☐ Listen without thinking what you are going to say while your spouse talks.
☐ Use positive loving words even in conflicts.
☐ Seek to communicate fully with your spouse and understand his/her concerns.
☐ Look directly into your spouse's eyes.
☐ Have a pleasant facial expression.
☐ Body posture should be toward spouse.
☐ Sit near spouse.

You may want to ask your spouse if you can plan ten minutes together each day just to talk and share, each giving the other his complete, undivided attention. If your spouse has been used to your wanting attention and then giving it for periods of time halfheartedly, he/she may welcome a request for only ten minutes a day. And it will be more satisfying for you to have ten minutes of undivided attention rather than much more time in distant encounters.

Finally, as you do plan time for focused attention on each other, encourage each other with positive communication. Express your needs and listen to your spouse's needs.

3. Grow in communication skills.

Study and practice good communication skills. An excellent, practical book for improving communication skills is *Communication: Key to Your Marriage* by H. Norman Wright. It would be an excellent study either individually or together.

C. *Begin dating again (with your spouse, of course!).*

Remember the great times you had dating your spouse before you got married? Begin dating again! Set aside evenings to go out and be alone.

If your budget can handle it, go out once a week. If not, set aside one night every two weeks or once a month. You may find another couple who would like to also go out once or twice a month and exchange baby-sitting. Then your date nights would be free from baby-sitting expenses.

Next choose fun places to go. If your budget is tight, go to places that are inexpensive or free. Get a guide to what is happening in your area—museums, concerts, entertainment, restaurants, plays, etc. Sometimes you will want to be alone and other times you may want to double-date with special friends.

Your marriage can really grow as you take time for each other to build your relationship. It will not

automatically happen!

Focusing on your marriage relationship while the children are home is an investment in your future!

There *will* come a time when your children will be gone from home. If you have been growing in your marriage you will have a close intimate friend ready to share those years together after the children are gone. If you have not been growing in intimacy in your marriage during the child-rearing years, you may wake up after your children are gone and either be angry because of all the unresolved conflicts or be indifferent to someone you no longer love. Let's begin making practical applications in this area.

What have you been doing so far to continue to draw closer to your spouse?

_____

When was the last time that you and your spouse went out without the children? _____

Name four places that you would like to go on a "date" night.

1.

2.

3.

4.

Ask your spouse to list four places that he/she would like to go on a night out without the kids.

1.

2.

3.

4.

Circle any place that you both have listed and is a common interest. Consider doing this activity soon. If you have no common activities listed, share each other's areas of interest by selecting an idea from each list and taking turns doing what the other would like to do.

Talk to your spouse about the possibility of setting up a regular number of times to go out during each month. After the discussion, check how often the two of you would like to go out:

☐ Once a week
☐ Twice a month
☐ Once a month
☐ Other: _____

The most likely evening for us to go out is:

List two other times that are possibilities to also have time together to grow in your relationship (for example, after the children are in bed at night, or for breakfast before they get up on a Saturday morning):

1.

2.

We have suggested three ways to develop a growing marriage.

Which area do you feel you need to work on the most?

☐ Respect your mate
☐ Increase communication in your marriage by being positive and having more genuine encounters
☐ Spend quality, fun time together, without the children

In the space below write two things that you will do to make your marriage stronger.

1.

2.

There *will* come a time when your children will be gone from home. If you have been growing in your marriage you will have a close intimate friend ready to share those years together after the children are gone. Focusing on your marriage relationship while the children are home is an investment in your future!

SEARCH FOR TREASURE

NAME_____(50 POINTS)

_____ = 1 POINT
_____ = 1 POINT

ACTIVITY OR REWARD CHOSEN: _____

_____

DINNER FOR TWO

TO_____
FOR_____
_____

You have earned dinner out with
☐ DAD ☐ MOM ☐ A FRIEND
You choose the restaurant

SPECIAL ACTIVITY AWARD

TO_____ FOR_____

You have earned a special activity of your choice
DAY_____
ACTIVITY_____

SPECIAL FAMILY ACTIVITY NIGHT AWARD

TO_____
FOR_____

On_____night you can choose a special activity for our family._____

STAY UP ONE HOUR PAST BEDTIME AWARD

TO_____
FOR_____
_____
DAY_____

THE "I DON'T CARE TO WORK TODAY" AWARD

TO_____ FOR_____
_____

Redeemable anytime

YOU'RE GREAT!!!

_____
NAME

is awarded_____
_____

because _____
_____ .

Weekly Chores

Check one:
Plan A ☐ List tasks to be completed.
Plan B ☐ List rooms to be cleaned.

	Person Responsible

Daily Chores

NAME

MONTH

Before _____ A.M.	Before _____ P.M.
	1.
	2.
	3.

"Work hard and cheerfully at all you do, . . . remembering that it is the Lord Christ who is going to pay you. . . . He is the one you are really working for" (Col. 3:23, 24 TLB).

1st Week   1 2
M   ☐ ☐☐☐☐☐☐
T   ☐ ☐☐☐☐☐
W   ☐ ☐☐☐☐☐
Th ☐ ☐☐☐☐☐
F   ☐ ☐☐☐☐☐
S   ☐ ☐☐☐☐

2nd Week   1 2
M   ☐ ☐☐☐☐☐☐
T   ☐ ☐☐☐☐☐
W   ☐ ☐☐☐☐☐
Th ☐ ☐☐☐☐☐
F   ☐ ☐☐☐☐☐
S   ☐ ☐☐☐☐

3rd Week   1 2
M   ☐ ☐☐☐☐☐☐
T   ☐ ☐☐☐☐☐
W   ☐ ☐☐☐☐☐
Th ☐ ☐☐☐☐☐
F   ☐ ☐☐☐☐☐
S   ☐ ☐☐☐☐

4th Week   1 2
M   ☐ ☐☐☐☐☐☐
T   ☐ ☐☐☐☐☐
W   ☐ ☐☐☐☐☐
Th ☐ ☐☐☐☐☐
F   ☐ ☐☐☐☐☐
S   ☐ ☐☐☐☐

Chores completed and checked on time all week (except 1) = _____

'LEARNING TO CARE FOR MYSELF' CHART

NAME _____

Use this chart for teaching preschoolers to care for themselves and their things. List up to ten behaviors that you would like your preschooler to do each day. For example: brush teeth, wash face in the morning, get dressed, wash hands before each meal, put toys away when asked, put pajamas on, do not hit baby brother, etc.

At the end of each day give your child a star or check for each behavior that he did. Plan a special reward at the end of each day if your child has done everything on the list, with one exception. Later you can also add that the child do the behavior without being reminded. The child's chosen reward for each day this week is:

_____

	S	M	T	W	T	F	S
1							
2							
3							
4							
5							
6							
7							
8							
9							
10							

ANSWER KEY

Project 8, pages 25 and 26:

1. 1, 4	8. 7, 8
2. 2	9. 5
3. 3, 5	10. 6, 7
4. 1	11. 3
5. 1, 4	12. 1
6. 5, 6, 7	13. 7, 8
7. 2	14. 5, 6

Project 9, page 29:

The common denominator for all three examples was deliberate disobedience to a clear instruction and defiance of parents' authority.

Project 9, page 29:

Case Study 1: Problem areas: Mommy tried to bribe Melanie to be good; Mommy made a threat she couldn't or wouldn't carry out; Melanie, not Mommy, "won"; Mommy verbally attacks Melanie's personality, not her behavior.

Case Study 2: Problem areas: The broken plant is probably the result of an accident, not disobedience; Mommy's response is mostly venting her anger, not helping the children correct their behavior; the children primarily learn to stay out of Mommy's way when she's angry—instead of not to run in the house.

Case Study 3: Problem areas: Bill is old enough that other methods of discipline should be considered rather than a spanking, such as taking away the ball for a week (logical consequence); Dad embarrassed Bill by spanking him in front of a younger sibling; because Bill had to save face, there was no repentance.

Project 10, pages 32 and 33:

Logical Consequences:

1. Child cleans up the spilled milk herself.
2. Child has to come back and make the bed neatly before going to school or play.
3. Danny cleans up his tracks on the floor; Danny cleans his shoes.
4. Warn child that if you see the toys on the floor in the family room again, he will not see them for a week. If he does not remove them, take toys away for one week. Then return the toys to him after one week and state the same rule.
5. John is not allowed to ride his bike for a week.
6. No dinner and no snacks; child may not eat until the next meal; let the child serve up cold food for herself, eat cold food, and then clean up after herself, or child is not allowed to go out to play near dinnertime until she shows she is responsible to come in on time.
7. Ask the child to come back and close the door; if it happens over and over, tell child that the next time the door is left open, he will not be able to use the door and will have to stay inside for a while (amount of time should be appropriate for age of child).
8. Explain that there is one set of clothes a day and child stays inside until the clothes are washed and dried; child puts on pajamas and stays inside for the remainder of the day; or set a timer and have him come in once every hour to go to the bathroom.
9. Put Kelly to bed earlier if she cannot get ready for school in time; get Kelly up earlier in the morning; warn Kelly of the consequences that if she is not ready by 7:30 a.m. she stays home in her room all day with no playmates, no TV, no Mommy to entertain her, etc., or if the school will take action on tardy students, let Kelly get in trouble and pay the consequences at school.

Project 10, page 34:

Case Studies

1. 1, 2, 6
2. 3
3. None
4. 4, 7. The consequence of no special treats has no relationship to the misbehavior. You can relate the misbehavior to the consequence by not allowing Kim to play outside for a short period of time (1 to 3 days). A one-month consequence is unreasonably severe for a four-year-old.
5. 5

Footnotes

Project 1

1. Adapted from "What Kind of Parent Are You?" by Dennis Guernsey, in *Family Life Today,* © 1975 by Gospel Light Publications, Ventura, CA 93003. All rights reserved. Used by permission.

Project 4

1. *Help! I'm a Parent* by Bruce Narramore (p. 41). © 1972 by The Zondervan Corporation. Used by permission.

Project 8

1. From *Communication and Conflict Resolution in Marriage,* by H. Norman Wright (p. 6). © 1977 by David C. Cook Publishing Co., Elgin, IL 60120. Used by permission.

Project 16

1. From *Building Self-Esteem in the Family,* by Norman Wakefield, "Dimensions of Esteem" transparency for session 2. © 1977 by David C. Cook Publishing Co., Elgin, IL 60120. Used by permission.

2. Norman Wright, *Improving Your Self-Image,* © 1977, Harvest House Publishers, 1075 Arrowsmith, Eugene, OR 97402. Used by permission.

3. Test and rating scale from *Can You Love Yourself?* by Jo Berry, pp. 158, 159. © 1978 Regal Books, Ventura, CA 93006. Used by permission.

4. Adapted from chapter fourteen of *The Sensation of Being Somebody,* by Maurice E. Wagner. © 1975 by Maurice E. Wagner. Used by permission of The Zondervan Corporation.

5. *Ibid.,* p. 169.

Project 21

1. Dorothy Corkille Briggs, *Your Child's Self-Esteem* (pp. 64, 65). Copyright © 1970 by Dorothy Corkille Briggs. Reprinted by permission of Doubleday & Company, Inc.

2. *Ibid.,* p. 64.

3. *Ibid.,* pp. 64, 65.

Project 24

1. From *The Sensation of Being Somebody,* by Maurice E. Wagner (p. 34). © 1975 by Maurice E. Wagner. Used by permission of The Zondervan Corporation.

2. *Ibid.,* p. 75.

Project 26

1. From *Here to Stay, American Families in the Twentieth Century,* by Mary Jo Bane (pp. 24, 25). Copyright © 1976 by Mary Jo Bane. By permission of Basic Books, Inc., Publishers, New York.

2. *Ibid.,* p. 25.

3. *Ibid.,* p. 25.

LIST OF RECOMMENDED BOOKS IN TEXT

Ford, Edward & Robert L. Zorn, *Why be Lonely* (Niles, Ill.: Argus Communications, 1975).

Lakein, Alan, *How to Get Control of Your Time and Life* (New York: The New American Library, Inc., 1973).

MacGregor, Malcolm, *Training Your Children to Handle Money* (Minneapolis: Bethany Fellowship, Inc., 1980).

McGinnis, Alan, *The Friendship Factor* (Minneapolis: Augsburg Publishing House, 1979).

Missildine, W. Hugh, *Your Inner Child of the Past* (New York: Simon and Schuster, 1963).

Mitchell, C. C., *Let's Live* (Old Tappan, N.J.: Fleming H. Revell, Calif.: 1975).

Narramore, Bruce and Bill Counts, *Freedom from Guilt* (Santa Ana, Calif.: Vision House, 1974).

Narramore, Bruce, *You're Someone Special* (Grand Rapids, Mich.: The Zondervan Publishing House, 1978).

Swindoll, Charles R., *You and Your Child* (Nashville: Thomas Nelson Publishers, 1977).

Wagner, Maurice E., *Put It All Together* (Grand Rapids, Mich.: The Zondervan Publishing House, 1974).

Wagner, Maurice E., *The Sensation of Being Someone* (Grand Rapids, Mich.: The Zondervan Publishing House 1974).

Wilt, Joy, *A Kid's Guide to Making Friends, Handling Your Ups and Downs, Making Up Your Own Mind,* and *Surviving Fights with Your Brothers and Sisters* (Waco, Texas: Word, Inc.).

Wright, H. Norman, *Communication: Key to Your Marriage* (Ventura, Calif.: Regal Books, 1974).

Wright, H. Norman, *Improving Your Self-Image* (Eugene, Ore.: Harvest House, 1977).